A PROJECT BY HADASSA BEN ARI

THE HEROES
OF OCTOBER 7TH

HEROIC STORIES FOR CHILDREN

ILLUSTRATIONS: TEHILA BAR-HAMA

YEDIOTH AHRONOTH · CHEMED BOOKS

The Heroes of October 7th
Heroic Stories for Children

Editor in Chief: Dov Eichenwald
Editor, Children and Youth Literature: Adi Zelichov Relevy

Project manager: Hadassa Ben Ari
Online graphic design: Tehila Bar-Hama, Tehilula Studio
Printed version design: Gala Pre Press Ltd.
Public relations and social media manager in Hebrew:
Yehudit Damari Agassi
Content editing: Dannii Bernstein Mazor, Dr. Juliana Brown
Authors: Yonatan Ofir, Hadassa Ben Ari, Einat Barzilai, Yifat Gelbar,
Yehudit Damari Agassi, Moriah Harel, Rivki Goldfinger,
Naomi Toledano Kendal, Bar Manor, Yifat Noyman, Naama Frenkel,
Ora Polak, Dr. Allison Kupietzky, Rotem Ressler, Yael Shevach, Rachel
Shira Azrad, Shira Segal, Amitai Tinami, Efrat Kapach,
Baruch Kempinski, Hayim Eckstein, Hayim Schreiber, Reut Goldovsky.
English online project manager: Dr. Allison Kupietzky
Translations: Dr. Juliana Brown, Dannii Bernstein Mazor,
Rivka Ben-Yisrael, Dr. Allison Kupietzky
Psychological text advisor: Dr. Judith Sambol
English online editors: Joslynne Halibard, Dr. Juliana Brown

ISBN: 978-965-584-016-2

2024 Printed in Israel

For my team. What would we be without you?
Yehudit Damari Agassi, Tehila Bar-Hama and Shira Shimon.

For the writers, editors, translators, psychologists and all the
volunteers on this project. You made the dream come true.

To my own superheroes:

Shir-Zion, Baruch-Chai, Moshe, Miriam, Ahava,
Shalom and Ori-Shoshana.
My hand wrote and your hearts listened.

For Chanan, a hero from another planet.

For the heroes of our nation, and their families.
We will be better, for you and through your strength.

From the Editors:

Dannii and Joolz dedicate their work on the English versions of
our heroes' tales to two officers whose total dedication and love
for those under their command, and for Am Yisrael, was evident
even in their final moments:

Captain Shir Eilat Hy"d

Captain Yaron Chitiz Hy"d

"כִּי מִדֵּי דַבְּרִי בּוֹ זָכֹר אֶזְכְּרֶנּוּ עוֹד"

MAP OF THE STATE OF ISRAEL

HEROES AREN'T BORN OVERNIGHT

The Heroes of October 7th is a project which had its beginning in my attempt to help my children connect to what was going on in the State of Israel against a background of the war which broke out on October 7th, 2023, the Iron Swords War. We were being warned from every possible source not to expose our children to the horror stories, so what then would be ok to show them? After all, children always find a way to learn about things.

I asked myself how I could tell them the real story, how I could introduce them to the incredible heroes of our nation, who had emerged from the battle for their lives. Their greatness wasn't simply born overnight. They were the same people before these events, had spent their lives working on their midot (their positive attributes), and had absorbed the education with which their parents had raised them. Heroes are not suddenly born out of nowhere, and I felt that this was what I needed to tell my children. I felt an equal duty towards all those heroes who protected us and continue to protect us; simply to thank them.

We tell their stories in order to grow ourselves, and in order to raise the next generation on these values of friendship, camaraderie, giving, love and the warm Israeli-ness which all came vibrantly to life during this war.

I was joined by writers, graphic designers, editors, translators and psychologists who spent long days and nights working to publish a daily tale of heroism from the endless number of inspiring stories which the war brought to our doorstep.

Over time, widows and parents who had lost their children began to tell the stories of their fallen loved ones, so that their names would not be forgotten, and so that the entire world would learn of their bravery and courageous spirit. We simply couldn't stop.

Since initiating the project, each time I compliment my children for overcoming a challenge, and call them heroes, they hear the word differently than they did before. "If you had waited one more minute for your turn, instead of hitting, even though they pushed ahead of you", I said to one of my kids who was dealing with a difficult situation, "you would have added a new facet to your personality". There are exactly the sorts of stories I write about our heroes.

Choosing correctly and overcoming challenges is not always comfortable – but this is how heroes are born.

The war in Israel has shaken the entire Jewish world, and its effect is felt across the oceans as well. The anti-Semitism which has reared its head in unexpected places has served as a call to us to translate these heroic tales into other languages, in order to let Jewish children world-wide know that there is a tiny country in which Jews can always stand proudly, so that these stories may serve as inspiration for them as well.

I believe that in these stories, you'll discover yet another bond between the children reading and the source to which we are all connected – Am Yisrael.

With endless hope and prayers for a united Israel in times of peace,

Hadassa Ben Ari

HOW DO WE TALK TO OUR CHILDREN ABOUT OCTOBER 7TH?

As parents, we have a strong desire to protect our children.
We don't want to believe that they know the meaning of the words: terrorist, kidnapped, murdered.

Our children have heard about cruelty and death: most of them know what Pharaoh did to the babies of the Jewish people in Egypt. They also know what Haman planned in the Book of Esther and some of them, depending on their ages, have also heard about the Holocaust. But all this happened somewhere in distant history and doesn't threaten us now.

The horrors of the current war pounced on us as adults, and we are doing everything so that our children are not exposed to it, so they won't know.

It's worth stating it here: they know. They already know. If not from home, then from friends. If not from a reliable source, then from the Internet.

How do we maintain a balance between the need to protect a child and the important role of mediating reality in a way that suits them? We tell them ourselves, in a way that highlights the stories of heroism and sacrifice. So they too will strive to live and to give to others and to the people of Israel like those heroes, whose devastating deaths should not be in vain.

We translated these stories from the original Hebrew and then edited them after consulting with educational experts and psychologists. We are sharing their advice here:

- All of the entries in this collection include stories of heroism, strength, resilience, national unity, and hope. They teach the important values of helping others and rising above personal fears. Some of the stories also contain tragic information about individuals who were killed during the attack on Israel on October 7th or in battles during the ensuing war. While all of these stories need to be told, parents are advised to take into account their children's emotional maturity and developmental readiness to tolerate this difficult information when making decisions about which of the stories are appropriate to share with their children.

- What is important is not only the text of the story, but the discussion that can be had around the story. Ask your children what they think about the people and events in the story, and how the story makes them feel.

- It is important to validate the child's feelings about the story, letting them know that it is normal and ok to feel sad, frightened, and anxious about the events described and even about their own safety and mortality.

- While offering an honest portrayal of the attack on Israel, it is crucial to provide continuous reassurance to children about the protection offered to the people of Israel and worldwide Jewry by the IDF and other safeguards.

- Role-model a healthy emotional response by letting children know that you are also deeply saddened by the story but inspired by the heroism, strength, and resilience described.

- Make use of visual imagery such as a map of the State of Israel in order to help children better grasp the geographical factors associated with the attack.

- Maintain eye contact and physical proximity to children as you tell them the story. Young children may benefit from a hug of reassurance when hearing about traumatic information.

TABLE OF CONTENTS

RACHEL'S COOKIES

HADASSA BEN ARI

Rachel Edri from Ofakim is one of Israel's heroines. Do you know how she fought five terrorists and overcame them? By simply being herself!

Rachel Edri sells snacks and drinks at the Tze'elim army base, while also chatting and listening to the soldiers for a few minutes every day. After 42 years, Rachel has become used to talking to tough military men. Everyone knows that at home she is the perfect hostess, always welcoming guests in an exemplary manner.

On Simchat Torah, October 7th, a rocket siren sounded in the skies above. Rachel and her husband, David left their house for the nearest shelter. When they returned home they encountered five armed terrorists entering through the window. Before they realized what was happening, the terrorists forced them to go upstairs and Rachel and David became hostages. "We will release them in exchange for

the release of prisoners from Israeli prisons!", the terrorists shouted at the policemen who arrived at the house.

Rachel understood that she needed to buy some time to help the rescue succeed. "I have diabetes," she told the terrorists, "I need to inject myself with insulin." A terrorist escorted her downstairs, where she threw up and pretended to pass out. It didn't help, and the terrorist forced her to go upstairs again. During this time she managed to signal to the police how many terrorists were in the house.

For hours she kept her captors talking. She saw they were getting agitated and thought that if they ate they might calm down and not hurt her and her husband. She prepared them a good meal, and later served them coffee and cookies.

Meanwhile the policemen tried to stop the terrorists; one of them was killed and another was injured. Rachel bandaged the injured one and spoke to him warmly, "Eat something sweet, rest," and she put him to sleep. They sang her songs by Lior Narkis, an Israeli singer, and she sang them songs by Umm Kulthum, an Egyptian singer.

Rachel was very afraid, but she had faith that they would be rescued.

At 2 a.m. the police broke into the house, killed the terrorists and rescued Rachel and David. The rescue operation was successful thanks to Rachel's composure, patience, wisdom and hospitality. It's no wonder the entire country sees her as an inspiration.

OZ SAVES LIVES

ROTEM RESSLER

"Who are you?" asked the frightened girl from within the bushes. She had been hiding for hours with a few other people and repeated, "Who are you? A soldier? From the security services?"

"I'm from a nearby moshav," replied Oz, wiping sweat from his forehead with his hand, "take my phone, let your parents know you're alright."

Minutes later, in the van driving to safety towards Moshav Maslul, the youngsters eased the tension with non-stop chatter, unable to believe their luck. Oz listened to their conversation and smiled: "The terrorists were screaming at us 'Avraham, come out', because that is what they think we are all called!" The girl laughed and continued, "I almost crawled out," and everyone began to laugh with her. Oz took a look at them in the mirror, and marveled at their vibrancy and vitality.

"Goodbye to you all, I'm going to get more people," he said as he dropped them off at his home.

As Oz drove alone, without the sound of their laughter that had instilled confidence in him and a sense of togetherness, he continued on his way. He was very familiar with this road, which had now become dangerous. Until recently, he and his father had a farm in these fields, but after his father had passed away, Oz had been too sad to return. So he sold the farm.

In the distance he noticed armed figures on the road. He thought to himself, great, the army is starting to arrive. Slowing the car down as he approached them, he asked, "Are there any injured?" In Arabic they replied, "There are dead people". He instantly understood that these were terrorists, and at the same moment they realized he was a Jew! He quickly put his foot down on the gas and just managed to escape. He continued to the fields that he knew so well, to save more people who were hiding.

He no longer had to search the bushes, since his phone number had been passed on to others who were hiding and people were desperately sending him locations to come rescue them. He made numerous dangerous trips, from the early hours of the morning until late into the night, saving people. On his rescue mission, he encountered terrorists several times,but each time he managed to dodge them.

Oz Davidian saved one hundred and twenty people, with one small van. Oz, is not a soldier and not a member of the security forces; he is just an ordinary man. He is simply Oz.

IDO JOINS THE ARMY

YONATAN OFIR

Most of the residents of Talmei Yaffe – a small moshav (a cooperative community of farmers) near Ashkelon, have evacuated their homes temporarily. Only a few people who needed to stay remained on the moshav, like those who had to care for the farms. Many soldiers were stationed there too, to care for the safety and security of the Negev during the war. Of course all the children left, except for one child, whose name is Ido. All of Ido's friends left the moshav, but he had to stay with his parents, and did not have any lessons nor any after-school activities.

One day, the soldiers were playing soccer and they were surprised when a ball that flew off the field was returned to them by a young boy. The boy was Ido.

The soldiers invited him to play with them. Ido was very happy to join as he had been very sad and hardly left his room.

The next day Ido asked his mother to wake him up early, so that he could join the soldiers for their morning roll call. As Ido stood in line with the soldiers, they gave him a number, like every other soldier. And when they counted off and everyone shouted their number, Ido's young voice was heard shouting "twelve" and everyone knew he was part of the unit.

Since he had joined the roll call and already had a number, the soldiers decided to give Ido a responsible position – to be in charge of the medical equipment bag.. Ido was not only responsible for the equipment, he also learned about the medical equipment in the bag and participated in the unit's meeting. Since then, every morning Ido shows up for the soldiers' fitness training and every evening he joins them for dinner.

A few days ago the unit held a ceremony, and the soldiers presented Ido with the platoon's insignia.

And if you think that the soldiers did Ido a favor by including him, you may be right, but it is important to know that Ido also helped the soldiers a lot. Every time they saw him, they thought of their children at home, and of the children of the settlements around Gaza, and of children from all over Israel, and remembered who they are fighting for and who they are protecting.

A big thank you to Ido, who helped the soldiers to help all of us.

THE ALL-FEMALE TANK CREW

EINAT BARZILAI

Anyone who has ever seen a tank rumbling over the sand, whether in real life or in a film, is amazed by its power. In this war, the tank brigade, who have always defended the country's borders, shocked everyone even more, as the soldiers fighting from within the tanks this time were... female combat soldiers.

On that terrible Shabbat, the soldiers awoke to the sound of sirens on their base in Nitzana on the Egyptian border. They immediately realized that something huge was taking place; a real threat to the State of Israel. Karni, the company commander, woke Michal, the platoon commander. They gathered their squads and got into the tanks. There were four soldiers per tank; a driver, gunner, loader and commander. They headed out onto Route 232, on the way to the settlements around the Gaza Strip.

On the way, they noticed the hole which the terrorists had smashed through the border fence between Gaza and Israel and the swarms of terrorists going through it. They left one tank there to make sure no more terrorists could enter and continued along the road, firing the machine gun and shells at the terrorists. Commander Michal's tank stopped near the Sufa post. A tough battle was being fought there with the terrorists and Michal's tank joined our soldiers. Together they managed to clear the terrorists from the post.

Commander Karni's tank continued on towards Kibbutz Hulit, where there were a large number of terrorists moving among the kibbutz homes. Commander Karni revved up the tank's speed and BOOM! – she blew open the yellow kibbutz gate. Imagine a tank driving along the paths between the lawns and the kindergarten; paths meant for wooden baby carts and bicycles. The kibbutz was in danger and the soldiers fired non-stop.

The female tank soldiers battled for 17 hours in Sufa, Hulit and near the border crossing fence and they turned the battle to Israel's advantage.

Tal, Sara, Tamar, Ofir, Shaked, Michal and Karni are heroes. But they're not only heroes – they made history. This was the first time ever in the IDF, in the world, that women participated in battle involving tanks. If you ask your parents, they very likely know the song "HaShiryon Asa Historia" (The Armored Brigade Made History). Well, nowadays we could sing it again, because there is no doubt that the female tank soldiers will be written into the history books of the IDF and the State of Israel.

TEAM ELCHANAN

RACHEL SHIRA AZRAD

Menachem and Elchanan Kalmanson, two brothers, chat all the way down to the kibbutzim near the Gaza Strip. The brothers are close; both live in the same place – Otniel – and each one is a father to five children! Menachem is a little bit concerned about what's happening in the south of Israel, but is reassured by Elchanan. Perhaps reassured isn't the right word; Elchanan was focused on their task.

It began that morning, October 7th, when Menachem called up his brother: "Elchanan, did you hear what's happening?" Elchanan answered briefly and to the point, "I'm packing my things and heading down there. I'll find a way to be useful".

Neither brother was a soldier, and neither had been called up for reserve duty. They were just ordinary guys – fathers, sons, husbands, Israeli citizens – who realized that help was needed, and they went to offer it. Within minutes they were both in the car, not exactly sure where to head, but with a very clear goal in mind.

As they were nearing Kibbutz Be'eri, they received a call: "There's a girl in a safe room who needs to be rescued; her house is on fire!" They didn't hesitate to come to her aid and on the way, they realized that there were many, many more people who had been waiting hours to be rescued.

'Team Elchanan' moved quickly. They went house to house, searching for people. "Is there anyone here?" they asked, and an elderly lady answered, "who are you?"

"We're Elchanan and Menachem from Otniel. We've come to rescue you!" They helped her to exit the house, but not before they made sure she had everything she needed: her glasses, shoes, phone. They took really good care of her.

Their mission, rescuing the elderly and the young and anyone who needed them, went on for hours and hours. During the night, their nephew Itiel, their sister's son, also joined them. People were standing at the kibbutz gate, begging: "My daughter is still inside-can you rescue her?"; "My son is with his wife in their safe room"; "My grandmother is still in there". They understood their task; it was a race against time.

This powerhouse team of brothers and nephew entered the kibbutz over and over again to rescue more and more people. Incredibly, they saved one hundred people – one hundred entire worlds.

"This is what we were taught at home. If someone is in need, there is no choice but to help them", Menachem explained.

In the final house they entered, they encountered a terrorist. Their nephew Itiel came out unscathed, Menachem was injured but Elchanan, his brother, could not continue; he was fatally wounded.

Elchanan remains in our hearts, a reminder of the tremendous heroism that took place that day, all over this country.

MOSHE AND ELIAD, HEROES OF OFAKIM

BARUCH KEMPINSKI

"They will not take this joy from you, and in this joy, brother, I am with you", Nechi-Nech the Israeli artist sang.

Eliad Ohayon was a person who brought joy to everyone; even when occasionally down or sad, he still worked to bring joy to those in need.

Eliad volunteered with children with special needs. He filled their lives with his contagious joy; giving them love, playing, singing and dancing with them as though he were their big brother.

Eliad was assigned as Ofir Chai's 'big brother' in the volunteer group. When Ofir Chai passed away from cancer, Eliad wanted to do something special in his memory. He decided to build some wooden benches, and placed them in front of beautiful landscapes. He inscribed the name Ofir Chai on each of the benches, so that everyone who sat down to rest there would be able to get to know Ofir Chai.

Eliad had a good teacher; his father Moshe Ohayon lived his life giving to others. Both Eliad and Moshe were known for their acts of kindness within the Ofakim community, including hosting sick children from the Kav L'Chaim organization on Shabbat. Eliad's brother Amitai recalls "One day Eliad called me, and said he was going to buy a big station wagon. 'Why do you need such a big car?' I asked him. 'That way, I will have room for four children with wheelchairs', he told me."

On Saturday, October 7th, the Ohayon family and their friends hosted forty children from Kav L'Chaim.

Every Friday, in preparation for Shabbat, Moshe would send a picture of flowers from the yard to all his friends on WhatsApp. That Friday he took a picture of the yard full of children from Kav L'Chaim and wrote excitedly: "This time there are no flowers, but in preparation for Simchat Torah, we are hosting some special children. Our yard is full of glowing and smiling flowers."

The next day, when the sirens went off, Moshe hurried to get the children into the safe room in their home. Moshe and Eliad ran to help the neighbors who didn't have safe rooms. They went looking for the key to the neighborhood shelter, but when gunshots were heard, they broke into the shelter and quickly let the neighbors in.

At first they sat with the neighbors, inside the shelter. When they heard the sounds of battle outside, they felt they could not stay where they were. "Stay with us", one of the neighbors tried to convince them in vain. To everyone's dismay, Moshe and Eliad went out into the streets of Ofakim and were both killed fighting bravely against the terrorists and preventing them from harming the residents.

The flowers will continue to bloom, thanks to them and for them.

THE SHUKRUN SQUAD

YONATAN OFIR

"Get up! Get up! There's a war!" The company's deputy commander woke Uriel with a kick.

"Okay, okay", Uriel said, and rolled over onto his side.

The commander didn't let up. He shouted: "Something big is going on. By eight o'clock we're out of here!" Within minutes, Uriel Shukrun was standing in front of his soldiers, briefing them as they headed into battle.

"We're about to encounter something we've never seen before", Uriel told his soldiers on their way to the front lines. "There are terrorists in our settlements. We'll eliminate them all, rescue the residents, and evacuate them. Please send a message to your parents and tell them that everything is fine, then turn off your phones and get ready to fight in full gear".

Everyone listened, ready to follow him into the battle that awaited.

From that moment on, Shukrun fought alongside his soldiers, rescuing more and more civilians at each stop and junction.

From the Nirim intersection, at Nachal HaBesor, and all the way to Kibbutz Kisufim, Shukrun and his soldiers battled dozens of terrorists. They suffered severe injuries, saved many civilians, and did everything in their power to restore security in the south of Israel. At one of the intersections, the Shukrun team saw a van that appeared to be driven by terrorists. They killed them, and suddenly the soldiers heard shouts and banging noises from the trunk of the van. They hurried to open it, and out came a confused young woman who had been kidnapped from the party in Re'im. They evacuated her too.

From there, the team continued to Kibbutz Kisufim. As they began to search the area, they suddenly came under heavy fire. They were ambushed by terrorists who were hiding behind a wall. Shukrun's team suffered very heavy losses. As the senior commander on the battlefield, Shukrun directed the battle for hours. He continued to fight and make sure the wounded were evacuated, until he was hit. He was rescued in critical condition and flown to the hospital. This time he was fighting another battle; the battle for his own life.

Supported by his wife, who is also an IDF officer, Shukrun continues fighting to regain his strength and get back to full health, knowing full well that the difficult price he had paid enabled so many people – young and old, men and women – to live.

INBAL SAVES KIBBUTZ NIR AM

HADASSA BEN ARI

"Do you hear the sirens?" Inbal Rabin-Lieberman was the first person at Kibbutz Nir Am to realize that something was wrong on the morning of October 7th. Maybe it was the number of sirens, or maybe the strange noises she heard outside the settlement's fences that alerted her.

Inbal is not just any old member of Kibbutz Nir Am, where she grew up. As "Ravshatz", the coordinator of the emergency security squad, she has the very important role of being responsible for the safety of all the members of the kibbutz. She is the person responsible for the security of the kibbutz during any event, until the arrival of the IDF or the police. A role like this is usually taken on by older men with a lot of army experience. But even though Inbal had only a year's experience in the position, she was prepared.

When the electricity shorted following the sirens, she ordered one of the kibbutz members: "Don't turn the power back on!" He replied: "But you need to hear the news, you also need air conditioners." She repeated: "Don't turn on the switch, I hear suspicious voices and gunshots. I need an hour to understand what's going on".

Inbal thought of all the possibilities and, despite nobody asking her to do it, she quickly built a defense plan.

Inbal was among the first to understand exactly what was happening in the south with the outbreak of the war, and she moved with agility – she knew exactly what actions needed to be taken, right away. There's one simple rule to follow in a situation like this: prepare the Kitot Konenut, the armed, emergency civilian squads made up of kibbutz members, in case we need them.

Inbal went from house to house calling the members of the emergency squad. "Go and hide next to the fence!" she commanded them. "I ordered them not to turn the electricity back on, that way the terrorists wouldn't be able to break through the heavy electric gate at the entrance to the kibbutz."

Thirty-five terrorists tried to break into Kibbutz Nir Am that day but none of them managed to enter. All of them were stopped by members of the civilian squad and IDF forces. The resourceful, quick-thinking Inbal, the coordinator of ongoing military security, led the battle of Kibbutz Nir Am, saving the lives of hundreds of kibbutz residents.

THE CHILDREN ARE AS BRAVE AS SOLDIERS

HADASSA BEN ARI

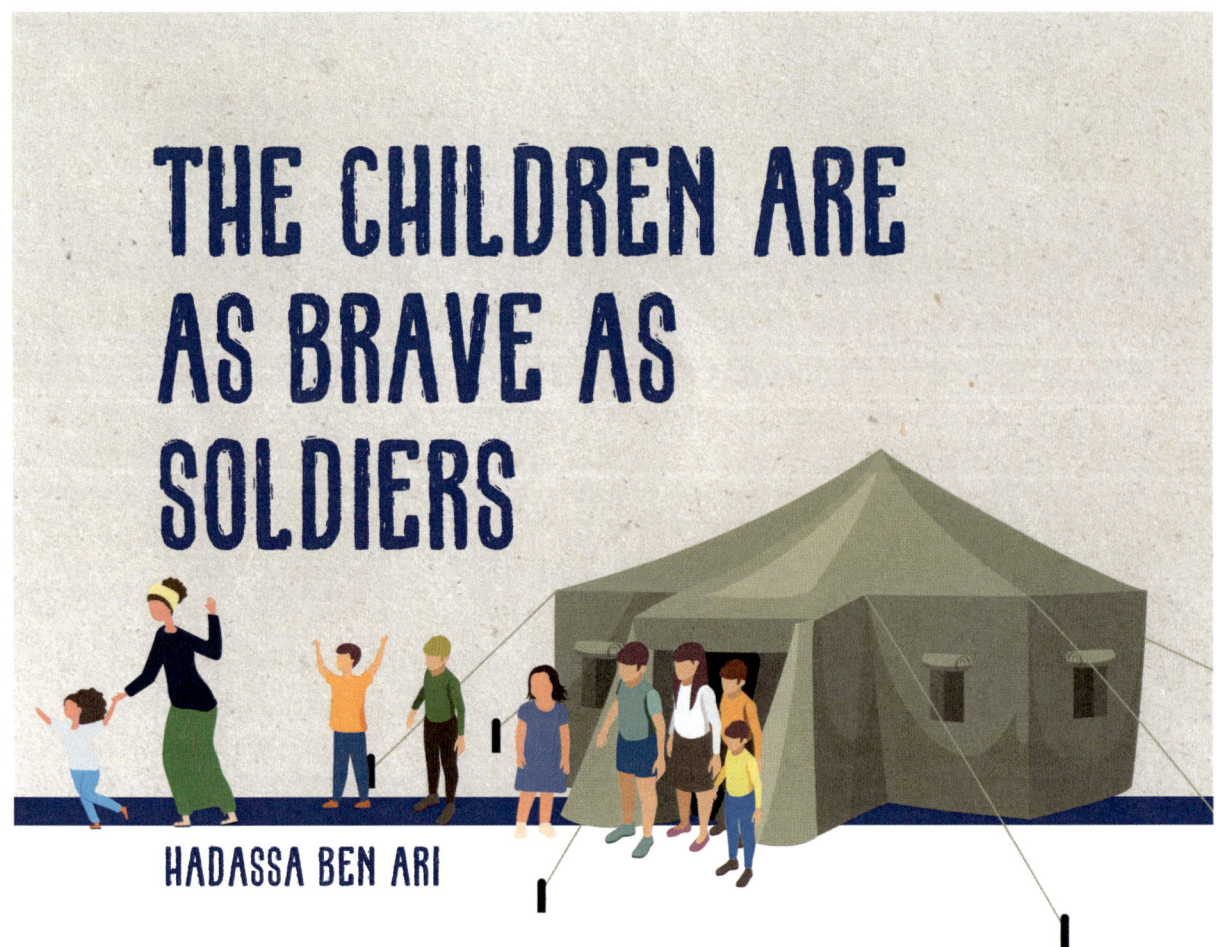

What were eight children doing at the Zikim base when the war broke out?

When Omri Alon informed his family members that they were going to celebrate Simchat Torah at an army base in the far south, not all of the kids were enthusiastic about the idea. But on Friday morning, eight of the ten children lined up alongside their parents and made the long journey from Kochav HaShachar to the Gaza border.

They were warmly received by the soldiers and fell in love with the place. When Tama asked what they should do if there was a Code Red siren, everyone burst out laughing. "Don't you see? The base is so close to Gaza. There is no way a rocket will fall here." That was a mistake.

On Shabbat morning, a little before 7 am, the sounds of "booms" were heard at the base. More and more sounds. Unusual sounds. In an instant, the heroic soldiers jumped out of bed. They fought still wearing their pajamas, holding their weapons while the children hid in a shelter together with their mother Michal. Time passed, and the explosions went on and on. "A soldier from the command has been injured," the soldiers cried. "Mom, you're a nurse, you should go help her," the children urged their mother.

While Michal was treating the wounded, another person entered the room. The devoted nurse thought he was coming to her aid, but no, he was a terrorist. He shot her and she was wounded too. More gunshots were heard in the air and wounded people began arriving at the shelter where the Alon children were hiding. Everyone was waiting for ambulances to arrive and help the injured. "Stay with us!" The children called to the soldiers, "Don't fall asleep!" As the children of a nurse, they knew that the soldiers had to stay awake until the ambulance came to evacuate them. They must not lose consciousness.

The children gave the wounded words of encouragement, singing prayers to them, saying Psalms and keeping calm, even though they too were afraid. When the rescue teams arrived to evacuate the wounded to the hospital, Omri, their father, decided to leave the children on the base and accompany Michal to the hospital. He knew Michal needed him and that the children would take care of each other and the soldiers. Two hours later, the children were brought off the base to safety.

Now the children of the Alon family from Kochav HaShachar understand why they were at the base on Simchat Torah: they were heroes themselves, and as brave as soldiers.

CAPTAIN H.: BEDOUIN SCOUT

NAOMI TOLEDANO KENDEL

"With cunning, you shall make war". King Solomon taught us this thousands of years ago, but here is one story of cunning warfare we could never have imagined happening today.

There are many Bedouin officers and commanders serving in the IDF. They are Israeli citizens who speak fluent Arabic, and among them are many military heroes.

One of these heroes is Captain H., who is known for his courage and professionalism. This is his story to tell. "I went out with my soldiers, and realized that there were settlements being invaded," he continued. "At this point, I thought for a moment that there was nothing more we could do here, on the Re'im army base. I could not even begin to imagine that the terrorists would reach us." Captain H. left the base and headed in the direction of the kibbutzim which were under attack and needed help, but when he reached the road there was no doubt in his mind what was actually taking place. "Suddenly fragments of bullets were bouncing off the road and hitting me." He fought fiercely and eliminated the terrorists. Captain H. then received an order to return to his base, where the soldiers would soon be in danger.

"We realized that only one side would win and we would have to do everything to be that side – it was either us or them," said H. He took off his uniform shirt, remained dressed in a white shirt and began calling out to the terrorists in Arabic: "Come, come to me!"

He said: "Not only am I fluent in Arabic, but I can also speak with the same accent as those from Gaza." As the terrorists came closer, thinking he was from their squad, he began shooting continuously, killing most of them and preventing the rest from taking over the base.

This wasn't the only time Captain H. saved lives that day. Later, he located 16 young people who had escaped from the music festival taking place near Kibbutz Re'im, and provided them with shelter, food and water. When H. was asked if he hadn't been frightened, or worried that he wouldn't return from the battles to his family, he stated clearly: "My job is to protect civilians and soldiers, so if that is what I have to do, that is what will happen."

AMIT THE PARAMEDIC

YEHUDIT DAMARI AGASSI

After her father passed away when she was only 12 years old, Amit Mann knew she wanted to help the sick and injured when she was older. The doctors who had treated him with such devotion helped her realize that this was her calling, to provide help and healing to anyone who needed it.

For years she waited to reach the age when she could begin paramedic training, to be one of the professionals who perform CPR in emergency situations for MDA (Magen David Adom). Amit passed the training course with honors and ever since, served as a wonderful paramedic.

"It was impossible to sit with her in a movie or go out to a restaurant without a call from MDA interrupting everything," said Marie, Amit's sister.

"She simply gave up going out with friends and family, and every time the call came to save a life, she left everything and ran."

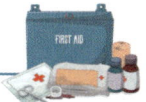

In the last two years, Amit had been the on-call paramedic at Kibbutz Be'eri. On the Shabbat morning when the war broke out, Amit woke up on the kibbutz. When the rocket sirens started, a close friend who was with her asked her to join him and leave the kibbutz immediately, but Amit refused to go. She knew she would be needed on the kibbutz and decided to stay. When she heard that terrorists had entered the kibbutz, she immediately texted her family that she had run to the dental clinic to be close to medical equipment, so she would be ready if wounded people arrived needing treatment.

Amit did not leave the clinic for seven hours. She treated the injured continuously and used every ounce of her strength to help, using the limited equipment available in the clinic. While treating the wounded, she tried over and over to contact the rescue forces to request assistance. Survivors from the clinic told Amit's family that her caring did not end after she applied dressings and distributed medication. They related how she encouraged and reassured them that they would be rescued soon, and she stayed right there, by their side, until they were rescued.

Our heroic soldiers arrived at Kibbutz Be'eri and rescued many people. Unfortunately, Amit was not granted the miracle of life which she gave the members of the kibbutz she had saved – but each and every one of those survivors who owe their lives to her, will never forget her, Amit the paramedic.

ITAI AND THE RESCUE OPERATION

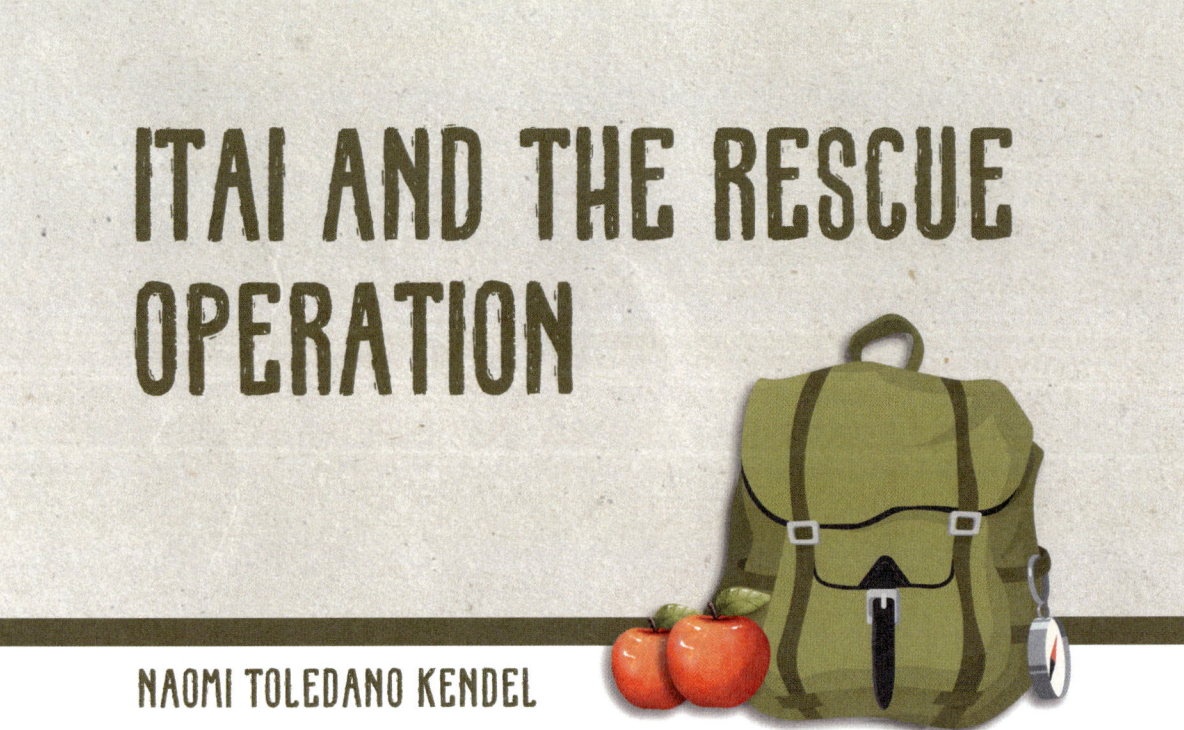

NAOMI TOLEDANO KENDEL

22-year-old Itai from Kibbutz Yavne was almost at the end of his active army service in the IDF. After years of being a combat soldier in the Duvdevan unit, he looked forward to returning to civilian life and made plans for the future. He went to the festival near Kibbutz Re'im on Friday night with his close friend Ben. On their backs they carried a bag full of apples and delicious sandwiches. The guard at the gate of the kibbutz couldn't understand why they were leaving home so late at night. Itai promised to bring him something sweet when they returned.

The party was exactly what they had hoped it would be – they danced, hung out with friends, and had a great time.

When the sun rose over Re'im, the sirens also started wailing. Shachar, Itai's father, tried to reach him by phone because he knew his son's unit would soon be looking for him to join the other forces in battle. But Itai didn't answer. In

fact, Itai was already in the middle of a battlefield. Without weapons and without a uniform, Itai was busy commanding an indescribable rescue operation for the dozens of wounded people crying out for help all around him. Itai the soldier knew what to do. Despite the many terrorists swarming the area, he showed the nearby policemen how to rescue the wounded under fire, directed the ambulances and other vehicles to safe evacuation points, and provided help to the victims, until he took his last breath.

During the shiva (the seven-day mourning period), survivors who owed their lives to Itai came to his kibbutz. Itai's parents heard from the people who managed to escape how he and his friend Ben returned again and again, even after they managed to get out of the danger zone, to help the injured and put them in ambulances.

"So many people told us that they saw him in videos running around, evacuating the wounded, offering help to everyone," said Itai's mother. About two hours after the fighting started, Itai left a message for his girlfriend Carmel. He wrote that he loves her and misses her and that his back and leg were injured. From that moment on, there was no sign of life from Itai. Eventually, his family was notified of his death.

Ben and Itai didn't return from the party they were so eager to attend, but many people's lives were saved on account of their resourcefulness and courage. They will never be forgotten.

SUPERINTENDENT SHIFRA BUCHRIS

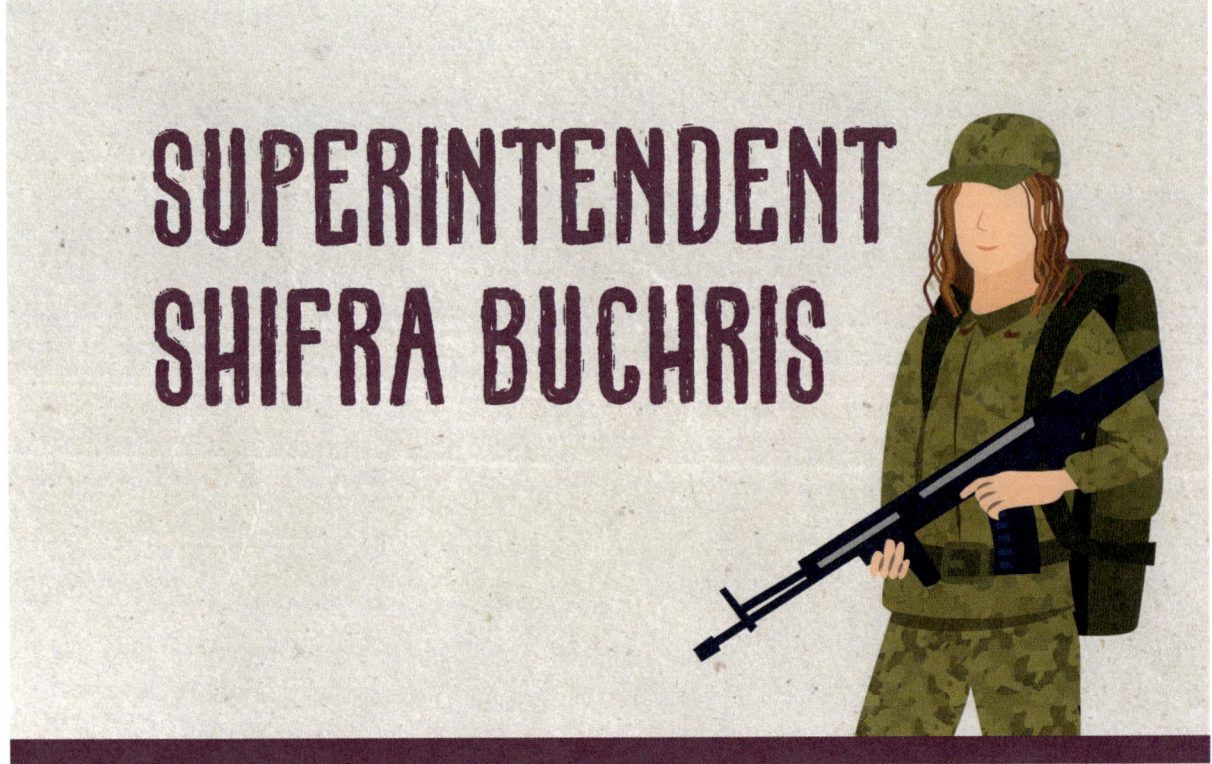

YONATAN OFIR

Shifra Buchris' ten children woke up early on Simchat Torah, in Merhav Am in the Negev, and discovered that their mother was not at home.

Superintendent Shifra commands the Border Guard patrol unit for the southern region of the country. She commands many fighters on a daily basis and early that morning, without receiving orders from anyone, she quickly realized what was happening and headed out with her lieutenant and two other policemen.

Shifra, along with another vehicle, drove towards Re'im where there had been a festival happening and where the terrorists had invaded. In the blink of an eye, thousands of concert goers found themselves caught up in a battlefield and Shifra and her friends knew that all those young people needed to be rescued from the terrorists.

For eleven hours Shifra and her team drove under continuous fire, risking their lives, to help get dozens of young people out of danger, to a safe place. Each time they evacuated one group from the area of the attack, the Border Guards turned around and rushed back to the area surrounding the festival grounds to help more people waiting to be saved.

Shifra and the other policemen escaped dozens of terrorists, passing them again and again on their way to the survivors. They flew over the bumpy dirt roads, with one goal in mind; to save more and more people.

"I'm a fighter in my soul," said Shifra, "but I decided that rather than fight, I would focus on the survivors. I decided to take care of the wounded and make sure they would be ok, so we didn't allow ourselves to delay by battling the terrorists." When they did encounter the terrorists, Shifra and the police caught them and handed them over to the army.

"I don't know if it has anything to do with the fact that I am a mother of ten children," says Shifra, "but the thought that something could happen to your child is one that no mother can bear. I thought about all the other mothers and one thing was crystal clear to me: my fighters and I needed to return as many children as possible to their mothers who were waiting for them at home".

Shifra gave life to ten children of her own, but she also gave many other children the chance to continue living their lives. This mother is a legend.

WHEREVER I'M NEEDED

HADASSA BEN ARI

On the morning of Simchat Torah, Naveh Lax of the elite Sayeret Matkal unit headed towards Kibbutz Be'eri. His phone rang, and his love, Shani, was on the other end.

"Naveh, where are you off to?" Shani asked worriedly.

"Wherever they need me", he responded with his usual answer, meaning every word.

At the end of his course in the commando unit, when they usually bid farewell to those soldiers less suited to be one of top fighters, the commander asked him: "What will happen if I get rid of you?" Naveh answered: "If I'm not suited to this, I'll go somewhere else, to whichever unit needs me". "Lax", the commander kept pushing, "It doesn't work that way. If I write that down on the transfer form, things won't end well".

How can I know where I'm most needed?

Naveh always wondered. For example, when he hiked along the Israel Trail, he asked himself whether to walk up ahead with the guide and listen to all the explanations about the archaeology and the history of the places they passed through, or to stay behind to help people who needed it. Most of the time he hiked up ahead, listening, and then headed back to help. And then ran ahead again, and back again, to help people having a hard time.

On the day the war broke out, his commander called him: "Lax, come to the front-line command room with me; we'll manage the combat from there."

"I'm not coming with you", Naveh insisted, "I'm going to fight." Though as a medic he could have remained in a safe spot to treat the wounded, Naveh went where he felt he was needed the most, and where his help would be the most valuable. This was the spot which all the Zionist heroes had spoken and written about when they fought; soldiers like Yoni Netanyahu and Dagan Vertman. He loved reading stories of combat history, admired the warriors and wrote about them in the diaries he left behind. Naveh joined the firing line, and the soldiers who rescued the kibbutz residents from their homes. During the fighting, he was killed by enemy fire.

Above his bed a small note remained in his handwriting: "Every day that passes will never return".

Naveh did not return, because he chose to go to where he felt he was needed the most.

NOA AND YOAV ARE GETTING MARRIED

RACHEL SHIRA AZRAD

Noa and Yoav had been planning their wedding for months on end. Like all couples, they waited for their special day with huge anticipation. They spent a lot of time working on the details: when the wedding would take place, where the chuppah – the wedding canopy – would be, what they would wear, how the tables would be set. They decided that their wedding would be held at Kibbutz Be'eri shortly after the holidays. The weather would be perfect in October and the chuppah would be backlit with soft, beautiful light.

On the morning of the festival of Simchat Torah, Noa and Yoav were together in the kibbutz. When they heard the sirens, they rushed to their safe room and waited, as they always did.

Suddenly they received a message on their phones: "There are terrorists in the kibbutz." They immediately understood

that they needed to stay locked in their safe room and remain quiet. They heard shots. As time went on, the sound grew closer and closer. Their anxiety increased, but the messages on the kibbutz Whatsapp group were reassuring: "The army is on the way!" wrote one of their friends.

Noa chose to think positively, even when it became unbearable to be in the safe room for hours on end without food or water. At one point, Noa felt she needed some air and cracked open the window of the safe room for a brief moment.

Through the open window she could hear birds chirping. She inhaled as much fresh air as her lungs could hold. A small tear rolled down her cheek. "There is life. Life is continuing and will continue forever," she realized. The fresh air filled her lungs and gave Noa the strength to continue waiting.

After many long hours, they finally heard the voices of soldiers — our soldiers, soldiers who spoke Hebrew, soldiers who kept their promises. The soldiers escorted Noa and Yoav out of the kibbutz to a secure place. From there, they were sent to Kibbutz Ein Gedi, together with the surviving residents of Kibbutz Be'eri.

Noa and Yoav realized they wouldn't be able to have the wedding they had dreamed of in Kibbutz Be'eri. Instead, they decided they would get married on exactly the same date, just in a different place. Their chuppah would be held at Kibbutz Ein Gedi, with a stunning view of the Dead Sea.

From a place of deep pain and crisis, a new home was built by a wonderful, sweet couple, by two heroes who overcame evil. The entire kibbutz helped with the preparations, and their lungs were filled with fresh, new air.

EITAN: LEGENDARY HERO

HADASSA BEN ARI

"I can't climb this mountain!" someone shouted, breathless. Everyone around them was panting and gasping for air. It was a training exercise, a few tough days out in the field. They were filthy from head to toe and their weighty backpacks threatened to sink them into the swampy mud. Exhausted, wet and dirty, the soldiers continued to make their way up the mountain.

"Be careful not to slip!" shouted someone else.

The group were taking one step forward, three steps back. They have to finish the exercise in one piece, but their desperation is mounting. Suddenly, Eitan Na'eh spies a fellow soldier kneeling on the side of the road.

"What's wrong, bro? You've got to get up!" he encourages him.

"I really don't feel well, I can't keep climbing... keep going without me."

"No way!!" Eitan does not give up.

"The backpack is killing me, I just can't carry it anymore," the other soldier answers, almost fainting.

"Get up on your feet. I'll take it for you."

Eitan then moved quickly to the front of the line with not one, but two heavy bags on his back! To the amazement of his friends and fellow soldiers, he reached the top of the mountain first.

"It just wasn't possible," his friends say, "we don't understand how it happened."

Already in the pre-military prep school, everyone knew that Eitan would make it to an elite unit. And he did, he made it to the Duvdevan Unit, where he qualified for "Team 100", the elite unit of the patrol, where Eitan, the legendary hero, was their number one soldier. Eitan also broke Duvdevan's record in the Warrior Test – a test of physical fitness that tests how strong the soldier is. But he wasn't interested in the prize. "Dad, I won a prize, I can leave for a bit and come home," said Eitan, "but if I go out, then the rest of my team will have to be on duty for more hours. I'd rather stay and help. Is that okay?"

Only twenty six years old, Eitan was steadfast, daring and brave when he fought in the alleys of Gaza. And even then, his heart and his conscience wouldn't let him return home to rest, even though he fought for so long and was entitled to leave. Eitan died while defending his homeland, but the many, many stories of his heroism live on, and keep him alive in our memory. Eitan Na'eh, the legendary hero.

THE OFFICER WHO TOUCHED THE SKY

NAOMI TOLEDANO KENDEL

Sahar Saudien was only twenty one years old, but since becoming a combat officer of the Iron Dome Battery, she had repeatedly touched the sky.

Sahar, another name for the moon, was the name given to her by her parents Helen and David, but this Sahar was actually a star, whose heroism shone brightly.

During her military service and years as a soldier and as an officer, Sahar was part of the unit overseeing the powerful Iron Dome battery that we have all heard of – the one that launches interceptor incoming missiles into the sky, to prevent other missiles from harming the residents of the State of Israel.

On the terrible day when the Iron Swords war broke out, Sahar was on duty, although she wasn't meant to be. She had been involved in a car accident which had left her very sore and she needed rest in order to recover. But Sahar saw what was happening. She gathered all her strength, ignored the pain, said goodbye to her parents and reported to her army base.

The rocket fire that Saturday morning was unusual even for a skilled, experienced and professional officer like Sahar. Hundreds of rockets were fired from Gaza, non-stop, to cities in every region of Israel. Sahar and her soldiers launched thousands of Iron Dome missiles, touching the sky, shattering the rockets from Gaza into pieces.

When the battery's ammunition began to run low, she realized that they had to refill the launchers. Sahar and some of her soldiers left to collect equipment and were hit by enemy fire.

Having bravely fought the terrorists, Sahar, the girl named for the moon, was wounded and fell in battle.

On the morning that Sahar died, she had managed to repel hundreds of missiles fired at Israeli cities. Millions of people in Israel are totally unaware of the fact that they owe their lives to Sahar, the brightest of stars – the officer who touched the sky.

MY BROTHER THE HERO

YONATAN OFIR

"Everything I've done in my life, Ben had already done, because he's older", Natan says, smiling. "When we made aliya, it was the first time that we started something together. We studied together, worked together and went into the army together, and suddenly there was no one to consult or ask because everything was just as new for him."

In 2019 the brothers, Ben and Natan Kalinsky, left Sao Paulo in Brazil, and bought one way tickets to Israel. Ben was four years older than Natan, but they both came with a single purpose; to go into the army. They made sure to step off the plane right foot first, and the first thing they did was head to eat falafel.

The brothers grew up in far-off Brazil, in a Zionist family. Their grandfather Moshe, 94 years old, is a Holocaust survivor, and it was from him that they learned what Zionism was. Their father played them Arik Einstein and Shlomo Artzi songs.

The two brothers joined the local Tzofim (scouts) youth movement at Kibbutz Nir Yitzchak in the Gaza Envelope, and lived there for a while, in two adjoining rooms.

Ben was the first to draft and was accepted into the engineering and demolition company of the Nachal brigade. In the IDF, brothers are not allowed to serve together, so three months later, when Natan drafted, he was placed in a different unit of the Nachal, in the 931st company.

On the day war broke out, Natan, who was still doing his compulsory service, was told to return immediately from his holiday leave. Two days later, Ben joined him. He didn't wait to receive his reserves call-up order (tzav 8), but simply gathered his gear and headed south.

Because they both served in the Nachal brigade, they fought in areas close to one another and occasionally managed to meet up during breaks in the field.

On one of the first days of the fighting in the northern Gaza region, Ben identified a terrorist firing from within an orange house towards another IDF squad. He gathered his team and they managed to take out the terrorist.

Two weeks later, when he was out on a break and met his brother, he told him about the incident. "An orange house?" said Natan in shock. "So, you're the one who saved my squad!"

What a long road the brothers in arms traveled, from Brazil to Gaza, thanks to their Zionism and their love of Israel!

TALI EXPLAINS IT ALL

YONATAN OFIR

When things are explained to me slowly, I understand quickly! And I understand even quicker when my mom, Tali Versano-Eisman, is explaining. She explains why the sirens sound so suddenly, and why you need to pay attention to the instructions of the Homefront Command. She explains what can help that fear in your stomach to disappear, and also what helps so it doesn't come back. Maybe this is the same for all of you when your mom explains something – but with my mother, it's also a profession.

I'm not sure what the name of my mom's profession is, it's not exactly like 'engineer' or 'teacher' or 'doctor' but if you ask her she will say, her profession is "woman of resilience and a poet". Resilience is the ability to endure something, even when your surroundings are scary, and when the news and events that surround us are a bit stressful and worrying. Resilience is something you can learn and also something you can teach.

During the war, my mom does what she knows how to do best when she's wearing a uniform: performing a not-very-easy role for the army called "explaining the Homefront Command to parents and children". She goes to TV news studios and writes books for children and instructs parents on how to explain to us kids what's happening.

My mom knows how to make us feel better in the tense and stressful situation that surrounds us since the war broke out. She says that there are many ways to fight fear, and that the best of all is the ability to talk about it. We can talk about it with parents or friends, through writing – like short and optimistic poems (she writes some of these herself) – in meetings with experts, and also with hugs – lots and lots of hugs.

All of these methods also work when a stressful situation happens right inside your own home. For example, when we lose someone very loved and close to us, which is what happened to our family when our cousin, Ron Yehudai z"l, was killed on October 7th. When that happened, my mom explained that our resilience tools are our breathing, our good thoughts and listening to ourselves. These tools protect us from the inside, while we also trust those who protect us from the outside, like our strong army. And my mother. You should trust in her, too.

SUPERGRAN

YIFAT NOYMAN

Have you ever heard of a grandma who people would consider a ninja?

Yaffa Adar, grandmother to eight and great-grandmother of seven, never imagined that one day someone would write in the news that she was a Ninja granny or a "wildcat granny".

In her 85 years, Yaffa had accomplished so much; helping to found Kibbutz Nir Oz near Gaza, caring for babies and in the dental clinic and being an inseparable part of the kibbutz landscape. What is it about her that's so special?

On Simchat Torah, dozens of terrorists invaded the kibbutz and took Granny Yaffa away with them. She definitely wasn't interested in going with them, but she had no choice. They sat her on a mobility vehicle they found in the kibbutz and drove her into Gaza.

The terrorists had cameras which they used to document everything. They even filmed Granny Yaffa and the clip was broadcast over and over on the news. She's seen sitting between two terrorists with guns, with a big smile on her face. She's sitting straight, with her head up and her eyes are saying: I'm not scared of you!

Granny Yaffa was held in shocking conditions in Gaza; without the medications she needs and without the food she's used to eating. After 49 days being held hostage in Gaza, Granny Yaffa was returned to Israel by Israel's rescue forces, who had done so much to make sure she returned.

When she arrived, she had no idea she was so famous, or that her smile had given Am Yisrael strength, as if to say – we're strong, we will win!

When she was asked where she found the courage to sit like that in the vehicle and smile, with her chin up and a mischievous glint in her eye, she answered without hesitation: "Because of my children. I needed them to know and see that I was there for them. That I wouldn't break. Be proud of me! And I really did not break. I told myself that I wouldn't let them break me and I would never give them the pleasure of seeing me scared. I didn't cry or let any tears fall."

It's no surprise that when Granny Yaffa was released from the hospital where she was treated after coming home, dozens of staff with Israeli flags cheered her on with applause – exactly what a Ninja Granny deserved!

THE BROTHERS SHARABI

REUT GOLDOVSKY

Suddenly, a tank appeared.

Two brothers, Neria and Daniel Sharabi, were searching for a hiding place from the terrorists who infiltrated the Nova festival in Re'im on October 7th. They never imagined that this is what they would find – an IDF tank that had been driving on the road, veered off of it and stopped right in front of the Sharabi brothers! The tank had been fighting in the battle and was badly damaged and the soldiers inside were badly wounded, unable to control the tank.

Neria Sharabi was a fighter in the IDF reserves and Daniel was a combat medic in training. Neither brother knew how to operate a tank, but at this moment they knew – they were not giving up and were prepared to fight.

Daniel needed help from the army. He scrolled through his phone contacts and started calling anyone he could from the army, until he reached Yoni, who had served with him as deputy company commander.

Yoni immediately understood the situation and told Neria to look for weapons inside the tank. Yoni also began organizing a rescue force to come to their aid.

The brothers managed to find an automatic machine gun capable of firing hundreds of rounds per minute, but Yoni warned them not to waste ammunition. "Every 60 seconds – one round," he instructed them. Behind the tank and around them gathered dozens of party participants who had escaped. Neria operated the weapon and Daniel took command and assigned everyone a position. "From now on you are the general," he said to one of the other young men. "Congratulations on the appointment – shoot this gun!". Then the gun jammed. Neria knew that the gun needed oil to lubricate it, to release the bullet and continue firing.

But how could he search for equipment in a tank when the terrorists were shooting at them all the time?

Then Daniel had an idea – he remembered that at outdoor parties there's always wind, which dries out people's lips. Maybe one of the girls brought some sort of lip balm with them? He asked around and one of the girls in the back produced a bit of Vaseline from her bag! Despite the small amount, it was a miracle – the gun began to work again.

With the help of Yoni on the phone line, the Sharabi brothers fiercely defended the thirty young people hiding alongside them, until rescue forces arrived and helped all of them escape to safety.

MY NAME IS ABU RAMI

AMITAI TINAMI

The sirens that went off in Moshav Patish on the morning of October 7th, did not make Rami Davidian put down his coffee. After all, he was so used to hearing the red alert sirens in his agricultural town, they did not worry him.

Rami continued sipping his coffee, glancing at a message on his phone: "Please help my friends find their son, he was at a party near your house." Rami is a veteran farmer who knows the area like he knows the back of his hand. He drank his black coffee down and got into his car, completely unaware of the horrific events awaiting him.

Suddenly, he saw a swarm of people running away from a party. Young women and young men were running in every direction, followed by gunshots.

Rami had left home without a weapon and without any prior preparation. At that moment, he accepted his mission: "I need

to rescue as many people as possible as I can from here." He stopped for the young people who were running away, loaded them into the car, drove them to his moshav and returned to reload his car with young people. He maneuvered his car to evade the terrorists, and as he drove the winding roads only he knew about, he found escapees hiding in the wadis and ravines.

From the car, Rami called his family and friends on the moshav to prepare to take in and take care of all the Re'im Nova festival survivors.

Young people were running towards him shouting "Get us out of here!". "Get in quickly!" he said, but there wasn't enough room for everyone. Rami told them "Keep running behind my car and in just a few minutes you'll reach the moshav, there are people there who will take care of you!"

Many of the young people's worried parents were sent Rami's phone number. For four days, Rami carried out his mission. He drove to every hill and bush that he knew of in the area and rescued as many people as possible.

One of the locations he received as a rescue site was that of a young woman hiding in bushes. When he arrived, he saw terrorists approaching. Rami spoke to them in Arabic: "My name is Abu Rami. I am also an Arab. I came to warn you that the IDF is on its way here. Let's get out of here. You run in the opposite direction, while I kidnap the girl and escape to the other side."

They believed him and ran for their lives. In the meantime, Rami returned the young lady to her home. In addition to this girl, Rami rescued around 700 other survivors.

"Rami, we have no words! You are a hero of Israel!", the parents told him. Rami shed tears and said, in a choked-up voice: "I didn't want to be a hero, I don't need the honor. I did what a Jewish person should do."

INBAL – SUPERHERO TEACHER

NAAMA FRENKEL

If you've ever read a comic, you probably know that every superhero needs a secret identity, so that nobody would be able to guess that this person who looks so completely ordinary is actually Superman or Spiderman, and sneaks out at night to save the world.

Inbal Caspi has one of these secret identities.

Inbal, a teacher, is a woman who loves plants and children, and loves to teach classes on the sun and Planet Earth.

She doesn't have eyes in the back of her head like some teachers, but she has green thumbs that know how to take

care of plants properly – cleaning the root so it has air to grow, weeding weeds, giving a young seedling water, and many other secrets of those who listen to the soil. Her students know that in Inbal's classes getting messy is allowed – even desired!

On the morning of October 7th, Baruch, Kibbutz Magen's security coordinator, recognized the danger from afar and hurried to send the emergency team into the field. When she received the message from Baruch, Inbal's secret identity was revealed and she very suddenly turned from a gentle teacher into a fierce fighter.

Inbal immediately hopped on her bike and speedily pedaled over to the armory to meet up with Mano, her friend and teammate on the emergency squad. The small squad, all friends from the kibbutz, quickly spread out along the border fence, determined to protect the residents and stop any attempt at penetrating the kibbutz. Inbal and Mano positioned themselves at a strategic high point so that they could easily identify any approaching threat. Inbal took cover behind a large concrete block and readied her weapon.

"We see three terrorists running outside the fence, near Nadav's slide", she reported to the squad. A large group of terrorists had tried to enter, but Inbal remained calm and knew exactly what had to be done. The battle was long and difficult, and for hours Inbal bravely fought with her friends on the kibbutz against enemy fire. Together, they managed to repel the danger.

Inbal returned to teaching in her classroom, but now the secret is out – everyone knows that their gentle teacher with the green thumbs is also the superhero who saved Kibbutz Magen.

AMICHAI BREATHES ELSEWHERE

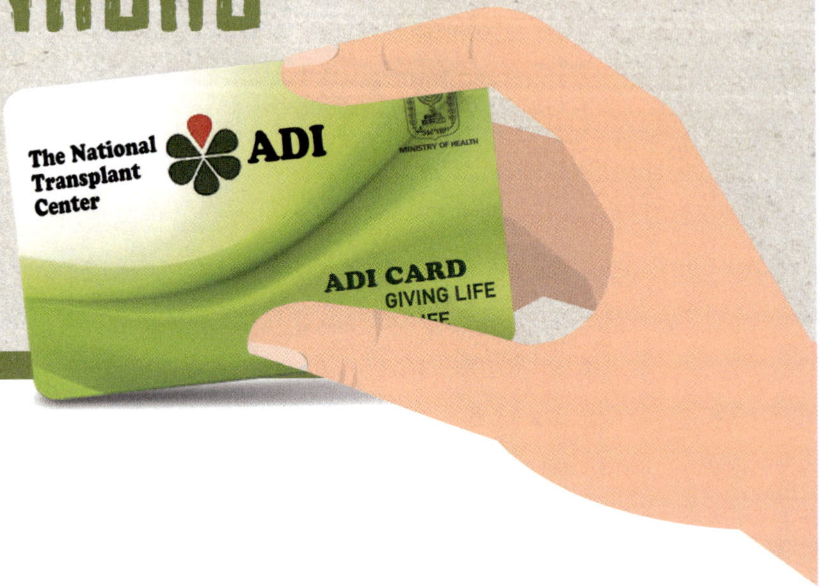

The National Transplant Center ADI

MINISTRY OF HEALTH

ADI CARD GIVING LIFE

YAEL SHEVACH

Did you know that a person can save a life even after his death? This is the story of the combat soldier Amichai Rubin from Akko. Amichai was always the first to volunteer. It takes a lifetime to build this desire and ability, and Amichai really knew how to volunteer. He was an outstanding soldier in the Golani battalion and was supposed to begin a commander's course soon.

When Amichai heard about the attack on Israel on Simchat Torah, he drove towards the fence separating Israel and Gaza and he and his friends battled many terrorists. He destroyed them with extraordinary courage.

During the attack Amichai was injured but he did not stop fighting. He continued to attack the terrorists alongside his

friends, providing aid to the wounded and protecting the soldiers who remained behind on his base. The battle was difficult and he faced waves of terrorists. After long hours of fighting, Amichai was injured and was rushed to the hospital.

With the same determination with which he had battled the terrorists on the fence, Amichai also fought for his life with the help of the doctors. In the end though, Amichai sadly died from his wounds. The doctors at the hospital where he was treated, together with his family, decided to donate his organs to other people in need of them to recover from medical problems with which they struggled. Thus, even after his death, Amichai continued to save the lives of others.

Amichai's lungs and kidneys were donated. The doctors also transplanted his liver into the body of twenty-three-year-old Aviel Ozan, who lay in the hospital, waiting desperately for a healthy liver that would cure him of his illness. Eight-year-old Rafael Horowitz was also able to receive a donation from Amichai's liver, and was cured of a serious illness and his life saved.

"This was Amichai," said his father Yishai, after meeting the boy Rafael, who is recovering thanks to Amichai's selfless donation. "He was good to everyone all his life. This is what made us decide to donate his organs. It was clear to us that Amichai would have wanted us to add life to the world and that's what we did."

MOSHE THE TRUCK DRIVER

ORA POLLAK

"Coffee break, guys! Pull all the trucks over for coffee!"

This time, Moshe Peled managed to get everyone to stop for a coffee break, before anyone else stopped them. "I'm making Turkish coffee for everyone; you've never tasted anything like this in your life", he says, working them up.

"Yallah, Moshiko, we're trusting you that this coffee will wake us up and give us the strength to keep driving", answered all the drivers in the convoy. So, they all sit by the side of the road, behind the trucks loaded with tanks headed south, and drink the best Turkish coffee of their lives.

Daily, they drive ten trucks south to north and north to south. When they have to, they also spend the night sleeping in the trucks on the roadside, and then continue on in the

morning. There are two soldiers per truck. When one gets tired, the other takes over the driving. These are soldiers from the army's Transportation Center. They're responsible for moving tanks, jeeps and Namer APCs to the areas where there's fighting. Imagine how difficult it is to tie down all these heavy vehicles onto the trucks with huge, weighty iron chains. And our Moshe is no spring chicken any more. He's 80 years old and has 14 grandchildren!

Before Moshe was a truck driver, he was a tank commander, and before that he was a paratrooper. This dedicated soldier did a lot of military service, took part in Israel's wars and its victories, but he just doesn't know how to stop. Anytime he felt that he'd fought enough and done his bit, he asked to be transferred to another position. Who could say no to Moshe?

He kept going and going until he reached the position he's in during the current war, Iron Swords, and if you ask him, this veteran soldier, he'll say that he loves being a truck driver, and that he keeps going despite the exhaustion and the challenges – because he knows that the combat soldiers are relying on him and on all the other truck drivers, to get the heavy vehicles where they need them, safely and on time.

Only in our country can you find soldiers who just can't stop volunteering for duty, even when they're already grandparents to many grandchildren and even great-grandchildren. May they continue to multiply!

YOSSI – THE SCHOOL PRINCIPAL

NAAMA FRENKEL

Yossi Hershkovitz was a special kind of dad.

He was a funny dad, who would often make videos on his phone that made you smile! He was the kind of dad who liked to get dressed up in really fancy costumes on Purim. He was a joker, the kind of dad who put cat-like meow sounds on his phone and left it outside of the family's Sukkah last year – the kids could not stop looking for the cat they just knew was hiding somewhere.

Yossi was the kind of dad who sat with his kids to talk about life and also lived life to the fullest. If he heard that someone was sick in the hospital, he would take his violin and play them music, to help the person regain their strength.

Yossi was also a school principal who cared about each and every one of his students. If he found a student outside of class in the middle of the day, he would carry him back to class via

piggyback. He was the kind of school principal who wanted every child to know how special they were, and to that end he introduced an app at school called 'A Good Point'. Teachers sent messages to parents through the app when their child did a good job in class, or did something kind or nice for a friend.

Early on in the war, Yossi was called up to the army. He served in a special unit of exceptional people, people who were ready and willing to leave everything behind to go and protect their country and their people. Every single soldier left his home and was ready to defend their country.

From Gaza, Yossi sent his wife and each of his children a letter. He also sent a video to his students and asked them to speak nicely to each other and to only say nice things about the people of Israel who do so much for their fellow Jews in times of war.

On a Friday, just before Shabbat, Yossi and two of his best friends bravely fought against terrorists, but they were killed in battle.

Thousands of people attended Yossi's funeral. They sang so many songs. His children told stories about him, and the violin that was played there reminded everyone that Yossi's special song, the song of a school principal, a father, and a soldier, will never be silenced.

If late at night when everything is dark, you look up toward the sky – you'll be able to see a shining light, or perhaps even many shining lights, that will remind you about all the goodness and light in the world.

In Yossi's words: "You just have to look and search for it".

https://www.israelnationalnews.com/news/381939 – link to a song that Yossi wrote in Gaza.

ELLA TRAVELS

NAOMI TOLEDANO KENDEL

@ellatravelsworld – that's how she is known by the many followers that Ella Kenan has on social media. A lot of people follow her blog and social media accounts as she shares recommendations for trips and experiences around the world, as a professional travel blogger.

When the war broke out and the information about what was happening was not yet clear, some information channels began to make serious accusations against the State of Israel. Despite the horrors of October 7th, the dangers facing the citizens of Israel were not receiving any exposure, while people posted their support for Hamas.

Ella realized that she had the power and the voice to change the image the world sees. She used her social media account

to show what was happening in Israel. Without an official position, without a salary and without asking anyone, Ella set out to tell the world the story of what was happening in the State of Israel and little by little she was joined by many others who took inspiration from her 'hasbara' – Israel advocacy – posts on social media.

Ella managed to crack the social media code to reach many more people around the world. Speaking in English, she spoke about the brutal attacks that took place on October 7th. She told the world exactly what Hamas were doing. She highlighted the stories of the hostages. Her words slowly worked their magic. They reached the right ears, setting in motion some powerful support for Israel from all over the world. Little by little, people began learning for the first time what really happened here on October 7th.

Ella's words reached some of the most important new outlets in the world, and many world leaders repeated the very words which Ella used to explain our reality. People with awesome graphic artist skills joined her, in order to help with visuals. Others, with influence in the world of the internet, helped ensure that the most important messages would receive the maximum exposure. Slowly, Ella became a 'hasbara' goddess; a travel blogger, a public diplomacy activist, and a hero calling out Israel's messages to the entire world.

GENERAL GRANDPA

NAOMI TOLEDANO KENDEL

The message that appeared on the cellphone belonging to Amir Tivon, a resident of Kibbutz Nahal Oz, as he sat in the safe room during a rocket barrage, filled his heart with hope. His 62 year old father, Noam, informed him that he was on his way to the kibbutz.

Noam Tivon was a general in the IDF (Israeli Defense Forces), a senior officer who had already commanded many battles in his life.

This battle, he knew, had to end in victory.

His son Amir, his daughter-in-law, and his toddler granddaughters, were waiting for him, besieged in the safe room in their home in Nahal Oz. All around them, rockets and sounds of gunfire could be clearly heard. Hamas terrorists had entered the kibbutz. While grandfather Noam was making his way to them, his tiny granddaughters Carmel and Galia

realized that they had to be quiet, lying in their bed, waiting. They were real heroes and managed to keep very still even when it was difficult and scary. Many hours passed. Heavy fears crept into the Tivon family's darkened safe room in Nahal Oz, but they knew Grandpa Noam would come.

Grandpa Noam's journey took a long while, as he saved the lives of so many people, even before reaching his granddaughters' house. He collected fleeing Israelis and drove them to a safe place, and then made his way again towards Nahal Oz. Later on, he joined up with a brave group of other soldiers he met along the way.

At the entrance to Kibbutz Nahal Oz, Grandpa Noam and the combat soldiers who were with him encountered terrorists in the midst of fighting other soldiers. They joined the battle, helped destroy the terrorists and evacuated the wounded for medical help. Grandpa Noam did not forget for a moment that this could only end when his family were safe, and so he returned for a third time to Nahal Oz.

When he arrived at the kibbutz, he joined the fighters who had already begun rescuing residents from their besieged homes. They went from house to house and helped dozens of people escape their safe rooms. After ten long hours, there was a knock on the window, followed by the voice of their Grandpa Noam, the superhero, who had finally arrived, after having saved so many other people on his way to rescue his own family.

LIEUTENANT LIOR RESTORES THE WAR ROOM

YIFAT GELBAR

The role of 'lookout observer' in the army is an all-important one that helps the IDF maintain safe and quiet borders. These (mostly female) observers sit in a Hamal (a war room), surrounded by computers and technology, constantly watching the border and reporting to their commanders if they notice something they consider dangerous.

A lookout observer's daily routine is divided into shifts, each shift lasts four hours, during which they must be hyper-focused! The soldiers must not take their eyes off the screen, or the area they are watching, even for a moment.

In the War of Iron Swords, the Nahal Oz war room and its observers suffered a heavy blow. On October 7th, many of the female lookout observers on duty that morning did not survive the attack. Some were taken hostage and the chamal (war room) itself was badly damaged.

That didn't stop Lieutenant Lior, a 22-year-old soldier, from cutting short her trip to Sri Lanka and getting on a plane back to Israel to re-establish the war room, this time a few kilometers from Nahal Oz, in a place called Re'im.

Lior put out a call for other lookout observers to join her, and to her surprise, almost all of them responded yes! The army also recruited hundreds of new soldiers for this important position.

At the entrance to the new war room in Re'im, the artist Liran Tapiro painted a gorgeous, moving mural. In it, you see three female soldiers standing in a field of sunflowers. The sky is blue, and the painting inspires a calm and hopeful feeling. Beneath the painting, the artist wrote the words "The flowers will continue to bloom."

Lieutenant Lior is also convinced that the flowers will continue to bloom, and that life will eventually return to some sort of normality. When she was interviewed for the newspaper, they asked if she was afraid to return to the position that claimed the lives of her friends. Lior answered:

"I wanted to go back. I was just waiting for the phone call to come back, because I feel that I have knowledge and experience that could help. When I see the number of soldiers that are here and their motivation to defend the country, I am not afraid. We have learned lessons from the past – we are strong."

It's thanks to people like Lieutenant Lior, who give so much of themselves, that we are as strong as we are.

NA'ARAN CHANGED THE RULES

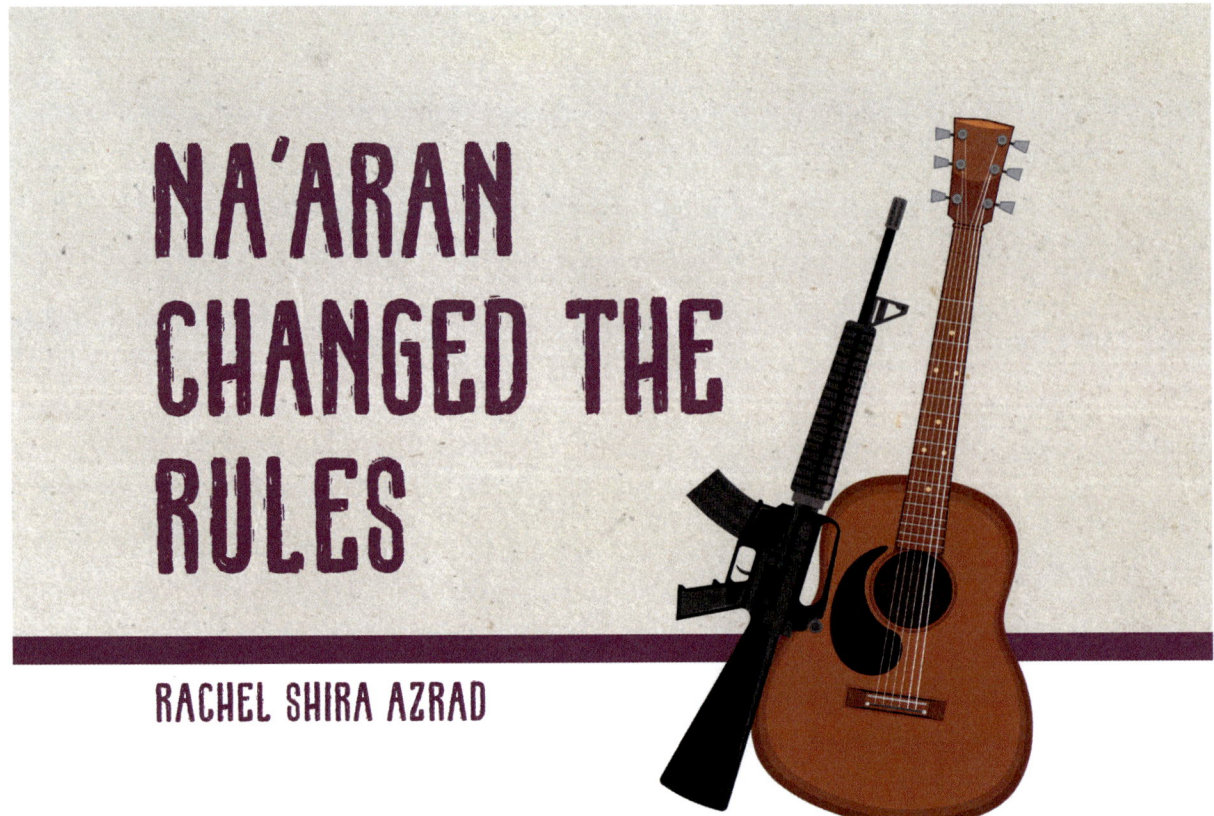

RACHEL SHIRA AZRAD

He wasn't even supposed to join this war. According to the official rules, Na'aran Eshchar didn't have to enlist in the army.

Four months before the war broke out, Na'aran donated one of his kidneys to someone whose own kidney was failing. Na'aran wasn't interested in knowing who the sick man was, he just wanted to do something good. He wanted to help, as much as he could, and if that meant having surgery and donating a body part to someone else so they'd be healthy – Na'aran was on board.

The war broke out just a few months after the transplant, so Na'aran wasn't eligible to be called up. This didn't deter him. He contacted the head of the transplant department to get special permission to return to active military service. He also went through difficult fitness tests to prove that he was fit for combat service. Na'aran passed the physical endurance

test and rejoined his fellow soldiers. They were thrilled to see him. Na'aran was everyone's friend – a good, kind man with a loving heart, willing to listen to others, and sensitive eyes that saw other people's pain.

When Na'aran headed out to his unit, he brought his guitar with him. When he sang his special melodies, everyone felt a little bit safer. Something about him instilled confidence in others and helped them believe that everything would be okay.

Na'aran and his fellow soldiers sat and played the guitar, they trained, they waited, trained some more, and waited more. Finally, the commander asked: "Who wants to bring round the tank to defend our position? We need a volunteer tank!" Na'aran and his tank crew immediately volunteered to go. It was a very dark night, and the road wasn't paved. During a sharp bend in the road, the tank overturned. Na'aran was seriously injured and was immediately evacuated to the hospital.

A week later, Na'aran passed away. During the week he was in hospital, people did good deeds, prayed and sang and were truly motivated to "do everything for Israel", as Na'aran had loved to do throughout his life. Even after his death, his family continued in the path he had set out on and decided to donate his organs. Four more people were given the opportunity to live, thanks to Na'aran.

According to the "official" rules, he should not have been called up to serve. But Na'aran never followed the normal rules; he always did his very best to help the people of Israel.

COMMANDER OR

ORA POLLAK

As a little girl, Or was scared of a lot of things. She was scared of dogs and didn't like being around dolls or stuffed animals. Once, Or went to an amusement park with her parents and there were enormous stuffed animals – she was terrified and ran and hid under a bench, until her worried parents found her.

Or's parents really wanted to help her overcome some of her fears, so they decided to get a pet dog. Little by little, Or learned to love her dog, and slowly she became stronger and less afraid.

When Or joined the Scouts youth movement, she was determined to overcome her fears. She wanted to be a leader. The same thing happened when she joined the army. Or was always first in line.

She was the first female soldier to join an all-male officer's course.

She was the first female commander of the Karakal Battalion.

She was the first one to fight and the first one to protect and take care of her soldiers.

The day the war began, Commander Or was at the base with her soldiers. When she received a message that a war had begun, and people desperately needed help, Or didn't hesitate for a moment. She led her soldiers to the battlefield, where, as always, she went in first. She was the first one to confront the terrorists. She was the first one to respond to requests for assistance, and she was first to reassure everyone she saw along the way.

Later, when Or was asked what was going through her mind when she first went into battle she said: "I was thinking about my children. I have three kids of my own and I have many more children too – all my soldiers."

Or's children are at home with their grandparents waiting for their mom to return from war. They are really, really proud of her. Their mom, who always makes sure to be first in everything, is also the first one to hug, kiss, and tickle them when she walks in the door.

Though Or used to be easily frightened and scared as a little girl, she chose to be brave and become a hero who always steps up first.

And if Or did it, we can certainly try as well.

NIRIT THE NURSE FROM KIBBUTZ BE'ERI

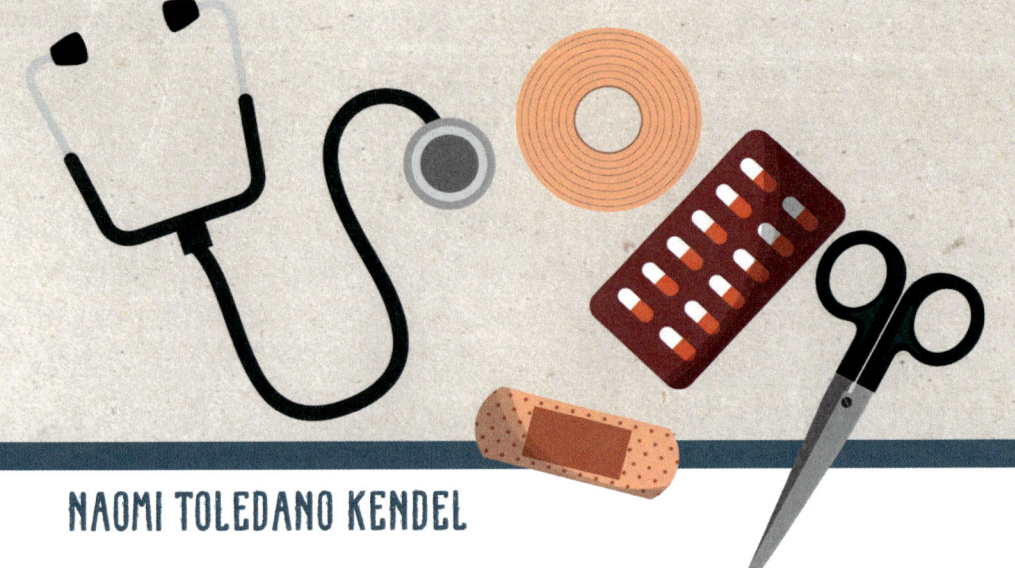

NAOMI TOLEDANO KENDEL

"I am always on duty – for everyone. I'm the nurse of the kibbutz," says Nirit Hohnwald-Kornfeld. Even on the morning of October 7th, Nirit was there for everyone, for all of the residents of Kibbutz Be'eri who really needed her during their darkest day.

"On Shabbat morning, at 6:30 am, the loud booms started. I hurried to get dressed, because I knew that if someone needed me, I would go that minute. Very quickly they called to say that there was a severely injured person near the dental clinic, and I ran to help." said Nirit.

Nirit came to help the first wounded man and realized that they needed to move to a safer place. A doctor who lived

nearby joined her and together they brought the wounded into the dental clinic, just as more wounded people began arriving in the clinic.

Nirit treated the wounded without stopping, gently and efficiently providing medical assistance, whilst all around them, kibbutz members were fighting terrorists. After many hours, the ammunition ran out and Nirit and her friends realized they had to hide.

Nirit worried that rescue forces would not arrive in time, but our soldiers did not give up, they continued to fight to get in and help. The soldiers did everything in their power to search for kibbutz members and bring them to safety. "After two hours in hiding, I heard voices in Hebrew: 'The IDF is here, it's the IDF! Is anyone there?' I had very little strength left, so I asked the soldiers to help me rescue my friends and family," said Nirit.

Even after she was rescued, Nirit did not abandon her kibbutz. With unimaginable strength, she re-entered the kibbutz with IDF forces to help save her family and friends from danger. She is one of Kibbutz Be'eri's surviving heroes – the compassionate and devoted nurse, Nirit Hohnwald-Kornfeld.

THE BRAVERY OF ANER SHAPIRA

HADASSA BEN ARI

Aner Shapira, a combat soldier in the IDF Nachal unit, was on leave for the weekend and went to a music festival, the Nova, located near the Gaza border. The Gaza border has a special fence with many IDF soldiers guarding it. That Simchat Torah morning, on October 7th, something very unusual happened. There were a lot of sirens and many Arab terrorists crossed the border from Gaza into Israel, entering the huge festival which was taking place in the fields next to Kibbutz Re'im.

Aner was quick and strong. He did not escape through the fields, but ran quickly to a shelter that is like an outdoor 'safe room'. About thirty friends from the party were crowded together in this space; Aner calmed everyone around him and told them that everything would be fine. He went on to tell them he was in a combat unit in the army and he would protect them. He listened to their fears and then gave each of

them a role so they would help him protect each other.

Aner announced that, "if the terrorists throw a hand grenade toward us (a small explosive that explodes a few seconds after it is thrown), my job will be to throw it back at them." And this is exactly what he did. The terrorists wanted all the people hiding in the shelter to come out or die. They threw a hand grenade inside and Aner threw it back at them. He did this over and over again – seven times.

"Look", he said to his friends nearby, "if the terrorists continue to throw hand grenades at us, you need to pick it up like this and immediately throw it back before it explodes." Aner, the brave combat soldier, was hit by the 8th hand grenade. He couldn't continue fighting and died in battle at the age of 22. Thanks to Aner, his friends continued to fight, and many lives of civilians and soldiers were saved. One of his friends said: "Aner Shapira from the Nachal unit saved our lives and he deserves an honorary medal. He was our guardian angel."

Aner's parents, Shira and Moshe, summed up his bravery in one sentence: "Aner found himself in a moment of fate and turned it into a moment of purpose." He didn't know he would be in danger, he didn't think he would die that day, but the moment he realised he was at war, he gave it his all.

THE TZITZIT THAT SAVED GUY

HADASSA BEN ARI

IDF soldier Guy Madar was not on his army base on Shabbat morning when the war began; he was celebrating the festival of Simchat Torah in another town, Kiryat Gat. When Guy heard that terrorists from Gaza were attacking Israel, he didn't even stop to change out of his festive holiday clothes into his army uniform – he immediately got into the car.

Guy managed to reach the war zone. He saw a seriously wounded Golani soldier nearby and carried him away from the battlefield to get medical attention. As Guy continued on his way, a terrorist shot in his direction but luckily, he wasn't injured. Finding a weapon lying on the ground, Guy managed to defend himself and deter five more terrorists. Like a scene from a movie, he found an empty police car, got in and began driving, all while terrorists were shooting at him. Guy was wounded but despite this, he kept driving and returned fire. His only aim was to save more people.

Eventually Guy had to abandon the police car and rolled into a ditch on the side of the road. His injuries had started to hurt; but from the ditch he continued to defend himself. Sheer exhaustion began to take over and his injuries were causing him a lot of pain. Guy was a soldier in the IDF, and he understood at that moment – he had to be his own doctor and take matters into his own hands. He put a tourniquet on himself and waited bravely and patiently for someone to come help him. He hoped he would not remain alone long.

After two and a half hours, ambulances arrived. When they saw Guy, he had a weapon in his hand and he was still wearing his festive holiday clothes and not his IDF uniform – they thought he was a terrorist!

Guy tried to shout with the remaining strength he had that he was a soldier, a Jew, but his voice was too weak to be heard. At the very last minute, almost before it was too late, one of the IDF soldiers shouted "Don't shoot, don't shoot! He's wearing tzitzit! He's Jewish!"

A few days later, on an IDF base, a Druze soldier was seen wearing tzitzit. "Why are you wearing tzitzit if you're not Jewish?" his fellow soldiers asked. He laughed and said, "Whatever protects you, will protect me too."

MAYA'S MEDITATION

YIFAT NOYMAN

Maya Alper is a dog trainer, but in recent years, she also learned breath-work – how to breathe correctly. She regularly practiced the breathing exercises, but had no idea that this new skill would end up saving her life.

Maya came to work at the Nova festival, a party that took place in nature, in the area where war broke out on October 7th. She had planned to travel for a month around the country with the money she would earn there.

While distributing garbage bags to her team to help keep the area clean, she still had time to admire the beautiful sunrise before the rocket barrage began and everything changed. Maya immediately realized that the festival, where only minutes ago hundreds of happy, joyful people had been dancing, had instantly turned into a battleground. She also understood that she would not be able to escape the area in a vehicle, so she hid in a bush, lying motionless, with the sounds of gunfire all around her.

In these moments of fear, Maya decided to return to the breathing exercises that had long since become a part of her life. She concentrated on her breathing, and fear began to give way to hope. "After a few hours in the bush, a bird sat on it," says Maya. "Suddenly I realized that the birds were still chirping, the sky was still blue, and I was simply grateful for the bush that protected me, for the sun that illuminated everything around me, for the wind that cooled me. I had no water, but I went back to breathing, to relaxing, and every time a hateful, angry or sad thought surfaced in my mind, I simply stopped and gave thanks – I thanked myself for making the right decisions thanks to which I am still alive, for being calm during this unimaginable situation. Every time a difficult emotion rose up, I realized I had to keep smiling. I was there for six hours in the bush, smiling."

When she finally heard voices in Hebrew around her, those of our soldiers, Maya cried "Help!" from within the bush, and they rescued her – she was safe and sound. With incredible resourcefulness, composure and a smile on her face, Maya was saved.

"This unimaginable situation taught me that every choice we make should be made with love and with a smile, even when it's very challenging," said Maya, who smiled in the face of incredible odds – and emerged victorious.

FROM HILLTOP YOUTH TO COMMANDER OF THE NAHAL RECONNAISSANCE BATTALION

BARUCH KEMPINSKI

"We need to talk," said Chaim to his son Yehonatan Tzur, whom everyone called Barnash.

Seventeen year old Barnash was incredibly sad. The summer before, 2005, the State of Israel had evacuated the Gush Katif settlements in the Gaza Strip. The IDF soldiers that Barnash had admired so much were the same ones who had evacuated the settlements, and his heart was broken. He loved the country so much, he moved to live on isolated hills with his friends to protect the country's lands. These young people are commonly known as 'hilltop youth.' Barnash became a hilltop youth. He got into all kinds of fights with local Arabs, which resulted in many police reports being opened against him.

"What, Dad?" said Barnash.

Chaim stroked his son's hair and said, "I know we are angry

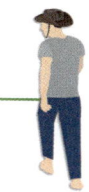

about certain things, but it is still our duty to serve in the army. It is wrong to harm our country because of anger."

His words affected Barnash, who decided to turn over a new leaf and channel his love for his country into a meaningful service in the IDF. Barnash clocked 1,000 hours of volunteer work in order to prove that he had turned a new page and trained intensely in preparation for his army service.

He arrived at the Special Forces Testing Day (the admission test for special units in the army) straight from the middle of a trip, in a cowboy hat and bare feet. He passed the test. Later, when he attempted to get into the Officer's training course and failed, he refused to give up. He tried again, and succeeded. Barnash eventually became the commander of the elite Nachal Reconnaissance Battalion!

"More than anything, he was an educator," said one of his soldiers. "After military operations, he would sit and chat with us instead of going to bed and regaining his strength. His connection to us was so important to him."

On the morning that the war began, Lt. Col. Barnash left his wife and three children at home in Kedumim and rushed down south to join his soldiers. "Orchuk, there are tons of terrorists on the roads; take care of yourself!" he warned Or Ben Yehuda, a commander of the Karakal Battalion, whom he had called up to report for duty.

On the very roads of the country that he so loved, Barnash fought with dozens of terrorists, thwarting their plans, until he eventually fell in battle. His heroic journey from the hills he loved through to his military service and defense of the country reflects his legacy – to do everything in our power on behalf of the State of Israel.

THE SOLDIERS' MOM

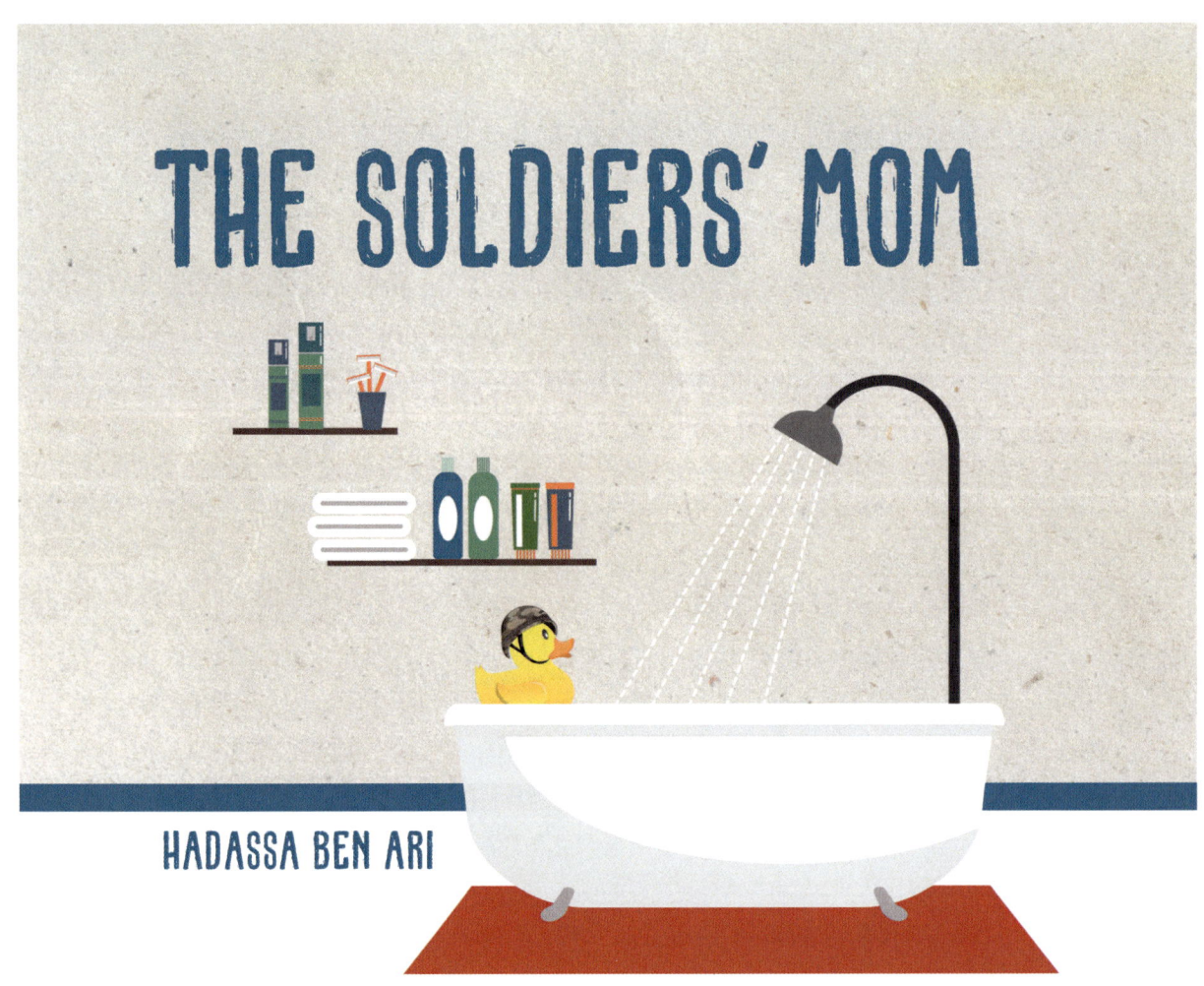

HADASSA BEN ARI

How can you not have heard of Orly Ezra? Orly Ezra is an angel. The guardian angel of the IDF soldiers in the north of Israel.

"I came to take a shower at Orly's, somewhere in a village in the north", writes Dori Gal, a soldier. "I heard a rumor that was going around among the soldiers that we could shower at Orly's house, and I decided to follow it up. I followed directions and got there, feeling a little shy. Her daughter shouted: Mom! There are three more here!"

Orly's house is always packed. Soldiers wander in at all hours, day and night. The kitchen is open around the clock, the vacation cabins she normally rents out are fully booked – with soldiers stopping by for a quick rest.

"This mom stood in front of me and was giving me a really hard stare", continues Dory.

"She knew everything – that I hadn't showered in a week and a half, she pointed out where my soldiers were positioned – she almost knew my exact coordinates! She gave me a big, motherly bear hug and then walked me through cabins and guest rooms packed with soldiers. We reached a cabin packed with army gear – uniform organized by size, army boots, and everything you could possibly need to revitalize a soldier. Orly looked at me and said: 'I'm getting you hair conditioner and a brush. Take an electric shaver and shave yourself, please.'

I showered, and emerged refreshed; like a new person.

Orly told me to go inside and eat. There was hot soup and rice, homemade pizza, salads, fried donuts, and eggplants. It was like a dream. I ate, I didn't dare not eat, and it was so tasty. I looked Orly in the eye and asked her why she was doing all of this. She told me she has sons who are combat soldiers in the army, and she had made the following agreement with G-d: you take care of my children, and I'll take care of yours."

Orly, the guardian angel of our soldiers in the north, has a saying, a guaranteed path to victory: "What do you need in order to move the biggest desert in the world, the Sahara desert?" she asks, and immediately replies – "for each person to pick up a single grain of sand."

MALI, THE POLICEWOMAN FROM SDEROT

RIVKY GOLDFINGER

"Mom, Dad, when I grow up, I want to be a police officer." This is what Mali, the little girl, would say over and over to her parents. Everyone knew that the day would come when Mali would wear a real police uniform and make her dream come true.

And that is precisely what happened. Mali grew up and joined the ranks of the Israeli Police Force. She loved her job as a policewoman. She spent thirty years working at the station and each and every day she felt the same excitement about the privilege she'd been given to protect the State and its residents.

On Simchat Torah, Mali left her home in Ashdod early in the morning. She said goodbye to her son Erez, and headed to work at the Sderot police station, just as she always did when she was on duty.

"Good morning!" she called out to her fellow police. It was six

twenty in the morning and time was crawling. 'Today's going to be so quiet', she thought to herself; a Shabbat that was also a holiday. While she was thinking about the day ahead of her, sirens began going off, one after the other. She and the rest of the police officers went into the shelter and waited patiently.

When the sirens stopped, she walked out of the station and noticed a truck full of terrorists in front of her. 'They want to take over the police station!' she immediately realized and knew that she and her friends would fight them with all their might.

The veteran policewoman quickly shifted into action. She ran into the station, calling to the others: "Hurry, there are terrorists headed this way! Grab your weapons and head to your post." They rushed up to the roof, taking cover in a spot where they had a good view of the terrorists. Any terrorist who got near the rooftop caught a hail of bullets from the highly-trained officers.

"Mali, grenade!" they shouted at her. She looked down and saw the grenade the terrorists had thrown at her. Mali knew it would explode in mere seconds, quickly snatched it up and threw it back at the terrorists.

The police officers of the Sderot station battled the entire day without giving in. Even when Mali was injured by terrorist gunfire, she continued directing the battle with immense courage. After eight hours the ammunition on the roof had run out and fighters from the police counter-terrorism unit climbed onto the roof using extension ladders from a firetruck. They rescued Mali and the other police, foiling the terrorists' plan to overwhelm our security forces.

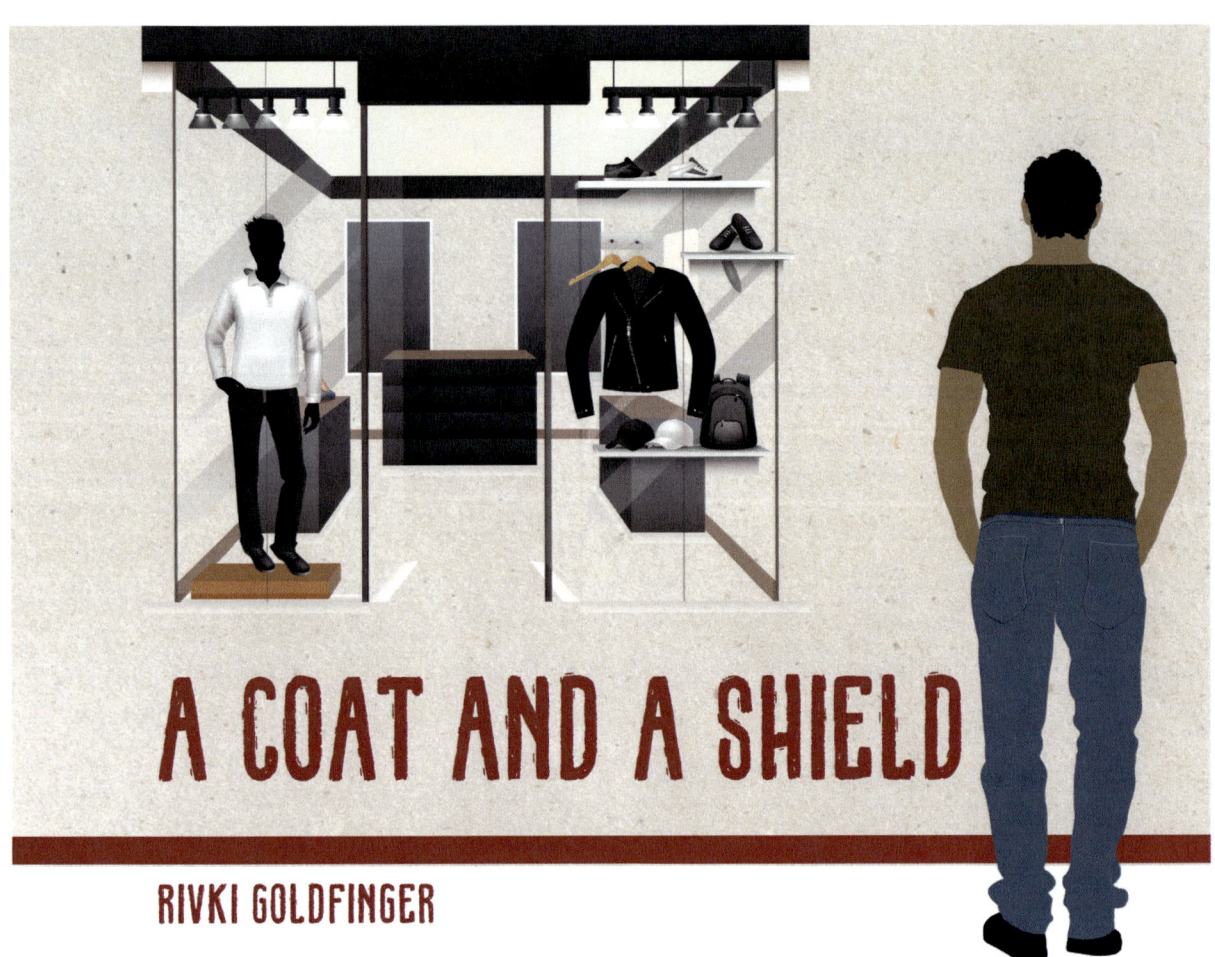

A COAT AND A SHIELD

RIVKI GOLDFINGER

Every time Yisrael Chana passed the store, he stopped to look at the windbreaker in the window. It was a warm, fashionable coat; exactly the right coat for his job as a security guard in the motorcycle unit of a bank security patrol. It was too expensive for his budget, so Yisrael waited patiently for the day he'd be able to buy it.

What Yisrael didn't know was that Shachaf, his girlfriend, had already bought him the coat! She wanted to surprise him and give him his dream coat on his 30th birthday, which came out on Shabbat Simchat Torah. Shachaf baked him a special birthday cake filled with whipped cream and bought him colorful balloons to decorate his room for the birthday celebration. She hid everything inside her car.

On the morning of his birthday, Yisrael and Shachaf went for a walk with their dog Marley. They walked to a beautiful park near home. Suddenly sirens started going off. They quickly ran to the bomb shelter next to Yisrael's house and waited patiently for the sirens to end.

Suddenly, loud gunshots were heard in the street nearby. "That sounds close," Yisrael said. In a determined tone, he said he needed to "go check what was happening" and rushed out to see for himself.

Yisrael cautiously peeked over the wall and saw terrorists in the distance. Immediately he knew what he had to do. Without thinking twice, he quickly entered the house, took his gun, and told Shachaf not to worry. Yisrael headed back out onto the street.

He moved from one hiding place to another, crouching behind parked vehicles and fences of houses and carefully sneaking up on the terrorists. When he was close enough, he opened fire and fought them for quite some time, all on his own. During the battle, he managed to deter one terrorist and injure another. Yisrael fought and fought and refused to give up until he was eventually wounded, and sadly died of his injuries.

Thanks to his determination, Yisrael was able to save not only his loved ones and neighbors, but also dozens of guests who had arrived at exactly that time at a nearby synagogue to celebrate a *Brit Milah* (circumcision) for a sweet, new baby.

Sadly, Yisrael never received the coat that would have protected him from the wind. He will always be remembered as the fearless protector of Ofakim's Mishor HaGefen neighborhood.

THE 100 YEAR OLD POET

HADASSA BEN ARI

In the home of 88 year-old Shari and 99 year-old Anadad Eldan from Kibbutz Be'eri – the walls are made of glass. That's the style you end up with in a house belonging to a Hebrew poet blessed with a creative spirit. Anadad published his first book of poems 65 years ago, and since then has written no less than 15 volumes of work. He wrote about the Land of Israel from his perspective – through the eyes of a fighter in the Palmach, as a combatant in the War of Independence, and later through the eyes of a farmer and a teacher on a kibbutz.

Anadad observed a newly emerging country as well as the birth and establishment of the State of Israel. In his one hundred years, he has witnessed history being made. But he never would have thought that in his very old age, he would be part of such an important war in the history of the Jewish people.

On the morning of October 7th, Shari saw what was happening in the kibbutz. Terrorists were walking around outside her house. They saw her, and she saw them. She didn't try to hide. How could she help her beloved husband go to the bathroom, for example, if she hid? Their caregiver had left two days before. Now everything was up to her, and she didn't want to let Anadad down.

Her initial decision was to not tell him about what was happening outside. He was already in a poor state, hard of sight and hearing, and with limited mobility, "but very assertive and very clear-headed," related Shari. He was her main priority and she didn't want to restrict his movement, so she simply spared him the details.

Anadad and Shari's daughter, Eshkar, worriedly called her parents. Shari told her she heard gunshots. "I wasn't afraid," recalls Shari. She didn't know everything that was going on at the time. "I probably have an internal mechanism that allowed me to disconnect, a survival mechanism that managed my sense of fear and let me function – I would even say function exceptionally well."

Shari felt that her job was to "take care of a hundred-year-old man" and she handled it perfectly, giving her the strength to get through the long hours until rescue forces arrived to lead the kibbutz survivors to safety.

PEDAYA'S LETTER

Dear family,

The People of Israel, and our family in particular, are facing challenging times.
We are strong! Am Yisrael are ~~ng. The IDF are strong.
~~ protect you and hold you in m~~ heart.
~~ill finish them off.
~~ll persecute my enemies an~~ ~~rcome them, and I will n~~ ~~ck until they are dest~~

~~e'll meet again soon, ~~ ~m Yisrael Chai.

Pedaya

EINAT BARZILAI

Pedaya Mark was already a hero at a very young age. When his father, Rabbi Miki Mark was killed, Pedaya and his siblings needed enormous strength to overcome his death. Despite this terrible hardship, they succeeded in remaining happy children. Another tragedy struck Pedaya when he lost his older brother Shlomi, who he admired greatly, in a car accident. Once again Pedaya gathered all his remaining strength and stood strong with his siblings. Pedaya lived in Otniel with his six sisters and three remaining brothers, who loved having fun with him. In the summer they would go to the seaside and sail boats, and in the winter they enjoyed breathing in the air and landscape of the green, southern Hebron mountains.

Pedaya was determined to follow in his older brother's footsteps. When it came time to enlist in the IDF (Israel Defense Forces), Pedaya had the option to serve in a non-combat unit. The State of Israel told the Mark family: "You have already contributed a tremendous amount," but Pedaya insisted. He was accepted into the Givati commando unit and even became an officer. The emblem of the Givati brigade is a fox, resembling the foxes of Samson, the hero who defeated the Philistines on the shore of ancient Gaza.

On Simchat Torah Pedaya went out to fight courageously with his fellow soldiers. They defeated many terrorists. He sent a letter to his family, writing that the days are indeed difficult but that we will overcome and win. He wanted to maintain an upbeat spirit for the soldiers and his family. On one of the days of fighting, the terrorists launched a missile that hit the vehicle in which Pedaya and his fellow fighters were traveling. Pedaya was killed along with several members of the crew.

It was a very sad, very difficult day for Am Yisrael and the Mark family. The family were asking themselves how they could overcome so much sadness, when they remembered that they had a letter from their Padushka, the nickname they gave Pedaya. In the letter, Pedaya asked them to be strong and told them he was doing exactly what he always wanted; protecting the People of Israel! Pedaya's brothers and sisters decided to be strong. And the entire nation of Israel embraced them from far and near.

THE BRAVEST DOCTOR

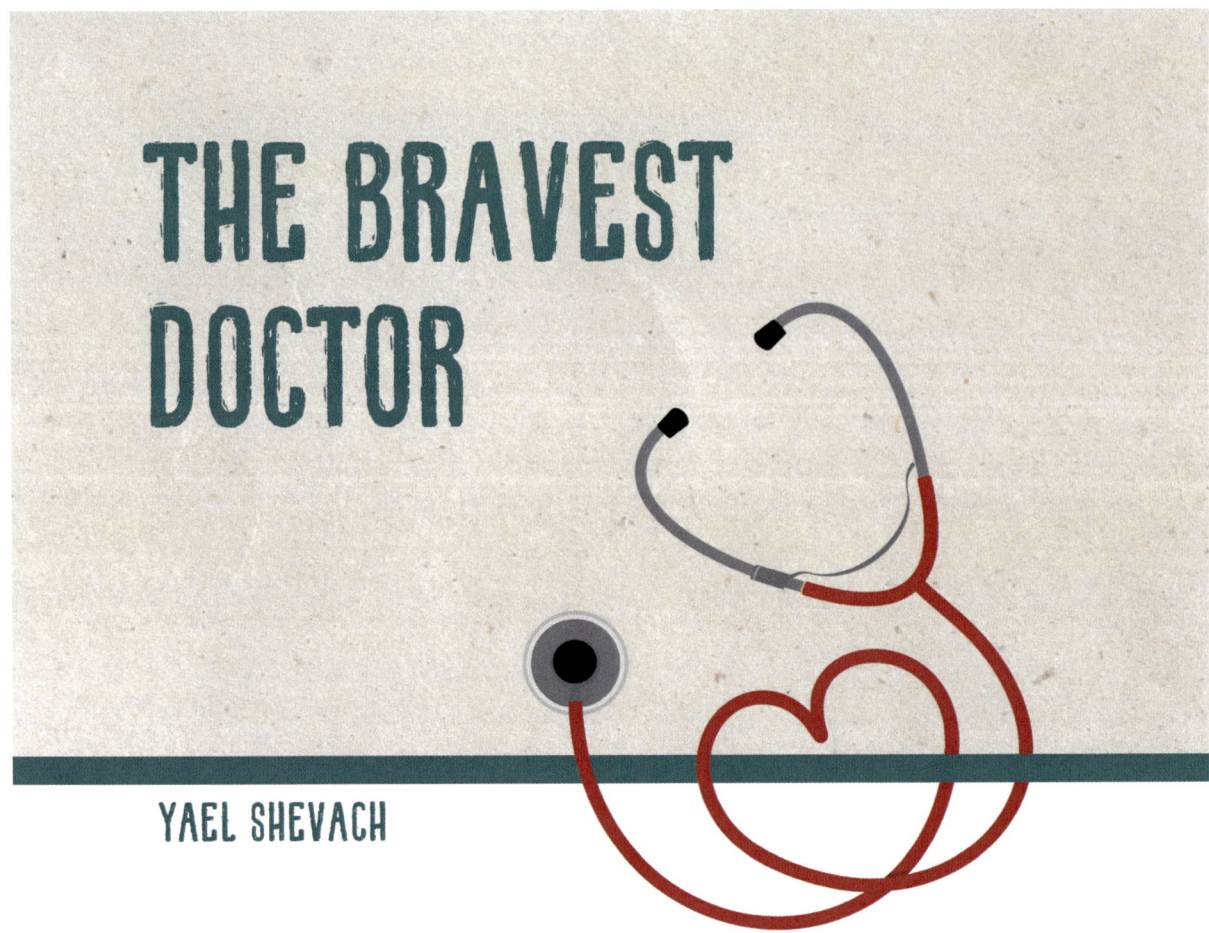

YAEL SHEVACH

Gal Grisaro from Kibbutz Zikim, near the border with Gaza, awoke on Simchat Torah, October 7th, to the sound of loud, incessant sirens. He knew he might be needed since he is a doctor, a medic in Magen David Adom and an ambulance driver as well.

Gal understood that this time something different was happening, something out of the ordinary.

The sirens kept wailing. Gal, his wife and four children remained in the safe room, inside their house – a routine with which they were familiar.

After a while, Gal heard their dog barking loudly. Gal decided to carefully go outside, crawling on all fours towards the fence. He found his beloved dog, having been frightened

by the sirens, stuck on the neighbors fence. With more and more sirens and explosions in the background, Gal managed to free the dog and crawled home.

Suddenly there was a power cut, and with the little reception remaining, they managed to keep in touch with neighbors and friends on the kibbutz.

One of the members of the security team, who are responsible for protecting the kibbutz, managed to call Gal and reported that some heroic members of the team had been injured by the bombings and they needed Gal to come quickly to treat and save them.

Gal debated what to do – should he leave his family alone and go out to care for the wounded? His brave wife told him: "They need you there. You have to go help them." Gal immediately left to treat the wounded in a special room prepared for that purpose. When he understood how seriously they were injured, he called MDA (Magen David Adom) to evacuate the wounded. Unfortunately, they replied they could not get close to the kibbutz because of the fighting and could not help. Gal called his older son, who is also a medic and lives on the kibbutz, and recruited him to help.

For five hours, Gal and his son treated the wounded with dedication and enormous effort, while under fire. In the end, they decided that they had no choice but to drive the injured to the hospital themselves.

Gal says that he was indeed responsible for helping the wounded, but for him the heroes were the members of the security team, who showed incredible bravery defending Kibbutz Zikim and all of its residents.

LAVI'S CAMERA

NA'AMA FRENKEL

Everyone would jokingly say that Lavi Lifshitz had two legs, two hands, a nose, a mouth and a camera – it was just another part of his body. He took his camera *everywhere*.

Twenty year old Lavi had named his camera 'Matilda'; it was black and beautiful and he would spend hours with it. He liked to look through the viewfinder, zoom out, zoom in, blurring backgrounds. But the moment he loved the most was clicking down on the button, capturing reality and framing it in a magical square that could be preserved forever.

When Lavi enlisted in the army, he decided to upload a photo every day that would describe one moment from the day, documenting him and his friends during army life. One day, for example, he snapped a picture from a very interesting angle of his friends all sleeping on the bus, and captioned it. He did this day after day.

Two years before the Iron Swords war, Lavi's camera 'Matilda' died. It happened during the pandemic, when everyone was in isolation at home. Lavi held a parting ceremony for her on Zoom (!) and everyone joined him on it, with both laughter and some seriousness, in memory of his beloved camera.

Lavi had a very good eye for photography, but also for people. He had such a sensitive heart that so often reached out to others. As a soldier during the Iron Swords War, Lavi took care of the foreign workers who were alone here in Israel. He also sympathized with the cows who were in pain because there was no one to milk them, as residents and farmers had been evacuated from the south. His concern for others knew no bounds, and sometimes – as he told his mother at the beginning of the war – he was heartbroken by the terribly sad things he had seen.

On October 31st, 2023, Lavi was killed in battle.

Among his things, found after he fell, he had written: "I don't regret my enlistment. It's something I'm grateful for. The ability to meet and find friends like the ones I found in the army is extraordinary. Thank you to our country that gave me this opportunity... I don't want you to wallow in grief. The action that can grow out of sadness can be so constructive. So I would ask everyone around me – always do, act, be constructive."

The next time you hold a camera, look for a moment through a lens that is filled with love for people and the world and take a picture. One picture, to fill the world with emotional, beautiful pictures. One picture, for Lavi.

OUR COMMANDERS ARE ALWAYS IN THE LEAD

BARUCH KEMPINSKI

"I'm really sorry, Roi", explained Golani Brigade commander Rasan Elian, "but you're going back to a command position! You need to focus on getting well!" Roi had been seriously wounded in the Tzuk Eitan operation in Gaza, when serving as a battalion commander in Golani. The doctors explained to him that with some time he'd be more or less back to his old self, but not immediately. "And what you need to remember", they emphasized, "is that you can't be a combat soldier anymore". But Roi wasn't about to give up. From his hospital bed, he continued to function as battalion commander. He gave out assignments to his soldiers, interviewed officers and even managed to complete a university law degree! The entire time, he was busy trying to convince senior officers in the army that they should let him go back into combat. To his great disappointment, they refused because of his medical situation.

After a long recovery period, during which Roi never gave up on his dream, he was assigned to be the commander of the IDF Officers School and later, against all odds, returned to a combat position and was assigned to command the elite Egoz unit.

A short while before Israel's 70th Independence Day, Roi received a phone call, informing him that he had been invited to light a torch at the annual ceremony. "I don't deserve this honor!" he insisted. "I'm surrounded by courageous people and heroes who are much more deserving of this". When Roi understood that it was not up to him, he gave in and was happy to light the torch in honor of all the soldiers who fought alongside him, defending the State of Israel. So, of all the soldiers, why was Roi chosen?

Roi once participated in a ceremony marking the departure of the American Chief of Staff, who asked Roi to tell his story. "There's only one thing I don't understand", commented the American, "how did such a senior officer get injured in battle?"

"In our army, the commanders are at the head of the troops", explained Roi to the shocked Chief of Staff. "Our soldiers get their courage from their commanders' brave example".

The spirit of the fighters remained foremost in Roi's mind during the battle for Kibbutz Re'im, on October 7th. He was wounded but insisted on ignoring his injury because he knew it would prevent him from continuing to fight alongside his soldiers.

Roi continued to fight and to rescue civilians until he fell in battle. And as for us, every time we find it difficult to stick to a task, or continue working towards a goal, we will remember Roi, draw on his strength, and continue taking one determined step at a time.

BROTHERS IN ARMS

BAR MANOR

On the morning of October 7th, Yishai Slotki's alarm clock did not ring. Instead, there were unending sirens, which sent his family and all the residents of Beer Sheva to their protected areas. In their building, confused neighbors gathered in the stairwell. The newsflashes alongside the commotion at the scene made it clear to Yishai that Israel was entering a war.

Yishai did not have time for morning prayers. He changed from his Shabbat clothes and put on his army uniform, taking his gun. He accompanied his wife Avia and their baby daughter, Be'eri Shachar, who was just two months old, as they went to a nearby building where his brother Noam lived. When they arrived, Yishai said goodbye to his family. His brother, Noam followed, bidding farewell to his wife Adi, and their son, Neta Yehuda, who was just 16 months old. Yishai and Noam were going to help protect the people in danger living near the Gaza border, the Gaza Envelope, which had been attacked by rockets and a terrorist infiltration.

The brothers left in two cars but managed to meet up and get into one car to go fight together. The long drive down revealed to them that the once pastoral landscape where they had taken many past trips for nature walks, had now become a battlefield. The brothers did not stop once on the dangerous drive, they understood that a brave heart was needed to protect the land and its people and a hero does not stand on the side when his Jewish brothers and sisters are in need.

They continued driving south, parked at a deserted bus stop in Kibbutz Alumim and then they charged forward.

The sirens were still sounding overhead as rockets were shot from Gaza at the Jewish farmland and kibbutzim but now there were also bullets whistling around them. Yishai and Noam fought a fierce battle, shoulder to shoulder, against dozens of terrorists who were attacking near the kibbutz fence. They waged an exhaustive battle against the terrorists, documented by their phone's GPS locations, and street cameras that filmed their courage and heroism, as the pair of brothers battled for hours.

That day, the brothers fell in battle together and their bravery will be always remembered.

On their final journey together, the honored soldiers were carried along many miles of streets in Israel lined with people holding the flag of Israel. The brothers united Jews of all types – religious, secular and ultra-Orthodox. All cried together with the Slotki family who had lost two heroic sons, who will forever remind us that we are all brothers and sisters, living together, shoulder to shoulder.

CAMILLE THE CAREGIVER

EFRAT KAPACH

Nitza is 95 years old and lives in Nirim, near the Gaza Strip. In recent years, as she aged, she began to feel that she needed a bit more help with tasks like cleaning the house and preparing breakfast. She decided to hire a woman to live with her and help out with all the chores she found too difficult.

Camille, a caregiver from the Philippines, has been living with her for five years. At first they had a more distant relationship, because they didn't really know each other, but over the years their relationship became much warmer and closer.

On the Shabbat when the war broke out, Camille heard a siren and immediately realized that they needed to get into the safe room. Camille loves Nitza as if she were her own mother, and since Camille didn't have time to prepare breakfast for her, as she ran past the kitchen she grabbed some cookies for Nitza. On the way to the room, she noticed a deathly silence, a quietness that alarmed her. For the first time since Camille had

arrived in Israel, she did not hear the birds chirping outside the kitchen.

Once inside the safe room, the noises from inside the house aroused Camille's suspicion. She heard voices speaking Arabic. Maybe these were the voices of soldiers? No. These were terrorists.

When Camille realized this she was very frightened, but instantly she decided that she had to do something to save Nitza. She came out of the 'safe room' and faced the terrorist. Her heart was pounding, but she spoke to the terrorist in the calmest tone she could muster and said to him:

"Sir, this woman is old and she does not understand what's going on. I ask you not to harm her."

Camille decided to give the terrorist her bag, which contained one thousand shekels. She also offered him her cell phone, hoping it would please him. The terrorist grabbed the bag from her and asked: "Is there any more money?"

Camille answered him in the negative. There was no more. Would he be angry? What would happen to her and Nitza? She was very concerned.

Miraculously, the terrorist was satisfied with the bag and left the house. Several hours later, the army came to rescue them.

Camille is a true hero; she is much more than a foreign worker, she is part and parcel of the family. Thanks to her love and devotion, 95-year-old Nitza was saved.

THE TIGER OFFICER

YIFAT NOYMAN

Yedidya Lev was a 'Namer' (tiger) officer. No, not tigers like on a safari or in Africa. A 'Namer' in the IDF is a type of vehicle. It is similar to a tank or an APC (armored personnel carrier); well shielded and very sophisticated. When Yedidya was first assigned to the job, he was a little disappointed. He had never really dreamt of becoming a 'Namer' officer, but he very quickly decided to change his attitude and learned to love the position, becoming the most skilled 'Namer' commander possible. Yedidya knew each and every part of the vehicle, including its power and capability. Yedidya knew that in wartime the 'Namer' would protect the fighters, when he led his soldiers into enemy territory.

Yedidya was loved by both his commanders and soldiers and they say that Yedidya's 'Namer' was impossible to miss. "Already, from a distance, we would recognize him because his vehicle was the most cared-for, decked-out, and always perfectly prepared", they said. Throughout the war, Yedidya and his soldiers received many letters and drawings from children all over the country, and Yedidya made sure to hang all the happy, supportive drawings inside the 'Namer'.

On one of the days of the war, Yedidya and his soldiers were asked to carry out an important mission inside Gaza. They searched and searched until they found a tunnel, where many enemy weapons had been hidden, as well as secret documents that helped defeat the terrorists in battle. With the 'Namer', Yedidya and the warriors by his side arrived at another battle scene. Yedidya made sure all the wounded soldiers were evacuated and that all his soldiers were functioning well, before he was hit and killed next to the 'Namer' he loved so much.

After his death, his parents had two requests for all those who wanted to remember the heroic Yedidya. Firstly, to learn from their brave soldier who made sure to call his grandparents every Friday and secondly, to ensure that the children of Israel continue to send pictures to our soldiers, to strengthen them and cheer them up just as they had made Yedidya so happy and had supported him while he was fighting in Gaza.

Yedidya taught us all a lesson in positive thinking and in total dedication – always seeing the good in everything, focusing on friendships and respecting one's parents and grandparents.

Yedidya's family name 'Lev' means heart, and that's exactly what he was – all heart.

SAVING PRI GAN

HADASSA BEN ARI

Benny Meshulam never imagined that he would need to choose between saving his own friends and neighbors, or saving the residents of the nearby community of Pri Gan. As the unimaginable crisis unfolded on October 7th though, this is exactly what happened.

Benny is the *Ravshatz* (the coordinator of ongoing military security) in the growing village of Shlomit. He is trained to face all of Shlomit's security needs and knows how to handle security threats and crises until the army arrives. Despite his experience, the situation that he faced on the morning of October 7th was exceptionally complicated.

On the morning of the festival of Simchat Torah, Benny began to receive reports that terrorists had infiltrated the neighboring village of Pri Gan. Pri Gan is an older community, and there are only two people in its *kitat konenut* – the emergency civilian squad that protects the moshav.

The emergency team fought bravely and stopped the

terrorists, but they didn't have enough manpower to keep things under control.

Benny hesitated: Should I go to help the people in Pri Gan? Or should I stay in Shlomit in case something happens?

He knew that the terrorists could reach Shlomit in a matter of minutes. Shlomit was filled with so many young families, and it was his job to protect them. Even so, Benny couldn't ignore the threat that hung over his neighbors in Pri Gan. He made the decision – Benny drove to Pri Gan with two of his friends and left the other members of the armed squad to protect Shlomit.

They quickly reached the neighboring moshav and began fighting against the terrorists. Six of the nine men who fought were badly injured. Everyone who was still able to fight continued to battle, until the enemy was deterred. Later, IDF soldiers arrived and helped evacuate the wounded.

The members of Shlomit's armed squad didn't have to go and protect Pri Gan that day, but they couldn't stop themselves. They were outnumbered and faced terrorists who were far better equipped, but the people from Shlomit were more driven and more determined. They were prepared to do anything and everything to protect, save, and support their friends and neighbors.

In courageously chasing the terrorists away from the area, they bravely saved seven different moshavim and villages. Just a group of heroes, who are first and foremost friends.

"I can't really relate to the term 'hero', because when push comes to shove, I'm just someone who was wounded," said one of the members of the armed civilian squad in Shlomit, "But I understand that on that day, we were, really, a group of heroes."

THE IRON FIST

ROTEM RESSLER

It was early morning, and Dvir Ressler, a Golani soldier, awakens to the smell drifting in from the fields. He thinks longingly of being at home for Simchat Torah and of the smell of his mother's schnitzels. He smiles to himself in resignation and gently wakes up Zvi and Azulay, his roommates, who simply turn over and continue sleeping.

This sleepy dawn is suddenly torn by multiple loud booms.

"Get up, get up," Dvir shouts, shaking them, "quick, come on!" The three of them race together to the nearest shelter. Dvir leaves his friends in the shelter, and runs to other ones nearby, to make sure that all the other friends are in a safe place. He thinks to himself – after a few minutes in the shelter we'll go show them that we mean business.

But the minutes drag on. And instead of hearing an all-safe siren, shouts begin to be heard in Arabic. Dvir suddenly realizes there is an infiltration of terrorists, and runs to the shelter door. The door doesn't lock but he refuses to give up, directing his two friends to hold the door together, while he stands closest to it. Dvir is very sturdy, whereas Zvi and Azulay are much lighter. He doesn't hesitate for a second, wraps his big fist around the handle and locks it in. Zvi and Azulay hold on to his hand. We are together, they tell him, knowing that his strength will endure for them, and wanting their friendship to endure for him.

And so, with an iron fist, all three of them brace themselves, determined not to give up.

Suddenly the handle moves. Voices in Arabic sound very close. Dvir signals to his friends to be quiet and tightens his grip. The terrorists increase their pressure on the handle, they threaten them, and kick the door. But the grip of these three friends is not broken easily. The terrorists think that with a little force they will overwhelm him. They don't understand that at that moment Dvir's grip is full of his love and concern for his friends. The terrorists don't stand a chance in the world of undermining this power.

After hours of stubborn struggle at the door, the unsuccessful terrorists decide to use an explosive to breach the shelter. The bomb explodes but the shelter remains locked. Dvir, who stood closest to the door, was killed but his friends survived.

His love for his friends saved them even in his death. The iron fist that saved his friends now becomes a never-ending story of loving friendship and deep camaraderie.

SAGIT SAVES KIBBUTZ EREZ

YIFAT GELBAR

On Saturday morning, October 7th, sirens were heard in Moshav Netiv Ha'Asara in the Gaza Envelope, but not in nearby Kibbutz Erez. Sagit Levy Gelfarb, a resident of the kibbutz, thought to herself: "How could it be? This is very strange."

Sagit is the head of the Community Resilience Team (*Tzachi*) in the kibbutz, which is made up of people whose job it is to be responsible when there is a danger or threat to the kibbutz. When necessary, the team gathers in a room to make plans – that room is called the war room (*Hamal*), and from there they manage the dangerous situation until the problem is resolved.

When Sagit heard the wails of the sirens from the neighboring moshav, she had an ominous feeling in her stomach. "Is it better to trust a gut instinct," she asked herself, "or ignore it and act as if nothing is happening?"

The decision was quickly made. Sagit sent a message: "All

members of the *Tzachi* team are asked to come to the *Hamal*, take weapons and radios and prepare for the possibility that we might be attacked. Everyone else should take shelter in the safe room (*Mamad*), close your windows and lock the doors of your houses."

Suddenly, Ben and Mai, high school students from Moshav Ge'a, who worked at the coffee shop in the kibbutz, arrived at the *Hamal*. "What should we do?" they asked Sagit, "Our home is far away."

"You stay with me," she replied.

And so, Ben and Mai sat in the *Hamal* and saw how members of the *Tzachi* team took vests, shields and weapons and went out to defend the kibbutz. A few minutes later, shots were heard near the fence. The terrorists tried to break into the kibbutz, but fortunately, thanks to Sagit, the *Tzachi* team was waiting, armed and ready, to defend the residents of the kibbutz.

Meanwhile, Ben and Mai sat alone in the corner of the room, scared. "I will take you to the safe room in my house and you will stay with my family," said Sagit. "We'll run across the grass to my house." And so they ran, under fire, while she protected them with her body.

Sagit continued to manage the protective force of Kibbutz Erez from within the *Hamal*. They successfully protected the kibbutz. After everything was over, Ben and Mai bought a large bouquet of flowers for Sagit and came to thank her. "You are a hero," they told her, "you saved us and the entire kibbutz."

"I'm really not a hero," she insisted. "I only did what you would have done too. I followed my gut instinct."

SHACHAR THE JOKER

HADASSA BEN ARI

"Could you please explain to me how it is that they placed you in the native English speakers' class?" Liat, the mother of Shachar Fridman, a native-born Israeli, wasn't sure whether to laugh or cry. Shachar had recently started 3rd grade in a new school, where they began learning English in 2nd grade. He hadn't yet had time to catch up on the material, but when the teacher asked him a few questions, he confidently gave the answers and was placed in the native speakers' class.

A week passed and the teacher called Liat. "I'm so sorry; there's been a mistake. Shachar isn't a native speaker". "No kidding!" laughed Liat. "I wondered when you'd catch on to that joker!" "What should we do with him now?", the teacher mused. Liat answered confidently, "Leave him there. Worst comes to worst, he'll learn to speak English".

The boy who had had trouble focusing in school when he was small, completed both English and Arabic with distinction.

Shachar learned Arabic from street cleaners. He made up stories that his mother was Jewish, and his father was an Arab, so they felt more comfortable speaking with him. He strengthened his Arabic by chatting with shepherds when he served in the army up north, and eventually became an interrogator. One of his aims as a soldier was to catch Arab shepherds who were spying on Israel. Shachar once wrote a note in Arabic: "Get away from here and don't even think of spying on us!" He inserted the note into the neck of a bottle and tied it to the neck of a sheep who ran off, straight to the shepherd. The IDF later adopted Shachar's method.

During the Iron Swords war, Shachar fought with the paratroopers, and before entering Gaza he texted a friend: "Read this, but don't show it to anyone else: Smile. Try to make everyone you meet smile too. Be open to criticism and always try to improve. Know that the greatest quality a person can possess is the ability to bring joy to others. Open your ears to the needs of others and open your eyes to their sorrow…"

Shachar lived these words his entire life. He made others laugh but was also extremely serious when it came to people with special needs; he would joke around with them, just as he would with any other child. They were his good friends and they eulogized him when he was killed in battle.

Shachar the joker was simply an unforgettable character.

"YOUR SONG"

YIFAT GELBAR

What do you do when you can't move or talk, but you can still think and feel?

Noa Ze'evi commanded IDF soldiers in basic training at the Zikim base. When red alert sirens sounded on the morning of Saturday, October 7th, Noa gathered her soldiers in a shelter and ordered them to remain there. But Noa herself did not hide. She came out of the shelter twice; the first time to make sure that a family with children staying on the base was evacuated, and the second time to help Ron, a commander posted at one of the nearby positions.

Noa saw the WhatsApp message Ron had written, saying they were being attacked, and immediately responded: "On my way".

Omri, Noa's best friend, had tried to stop her, but Noa refused. She put on her vest and helmet and bravely headed out. But Noa never reached Ron, as she was wounded and lost consciousness. Omri, who saw Noa injured, pulled her into a safe room, where she lay, quiet and weak. After what seemed like an eternity, Noa was evacuated for medical treatment.

This, however, is where the story of Noa's heroism actually begins.

In the hospital, the brave soldier lay in her bed. She was in critical condition and the doctors were not sure whether they would be able to save her. One day, however, a miracle happened – Noa moved her fingers, in a movement reminiscent of writing. Her mother, so excited, hurried to bring a pen and paper on which Noa wrote down two words: Elton John.

There was no end to the family's excitement. They hurried to play her favorite song, "Your Song", and Noa began moving to the rhythm.

A while later, Noa opened her healthy eye. A bullet had hit her other eye in the attack, but Noa merely proclaimed, "There are much worse things". She relearned how to walk and talk, and within days of waking she had begun laughing and singing again, as she'd always loved to do.

The hospital staff and all of Noa's friends and family supported her during her recovery, full of total joy and admiration for her. And when no one was watching, they all sang to her quietly, happily, those lyrics from the song that Noa loves so much: *"How wonderful life is, while you're in the world..."*.

OFEK'S LITTLE WHITE CAR

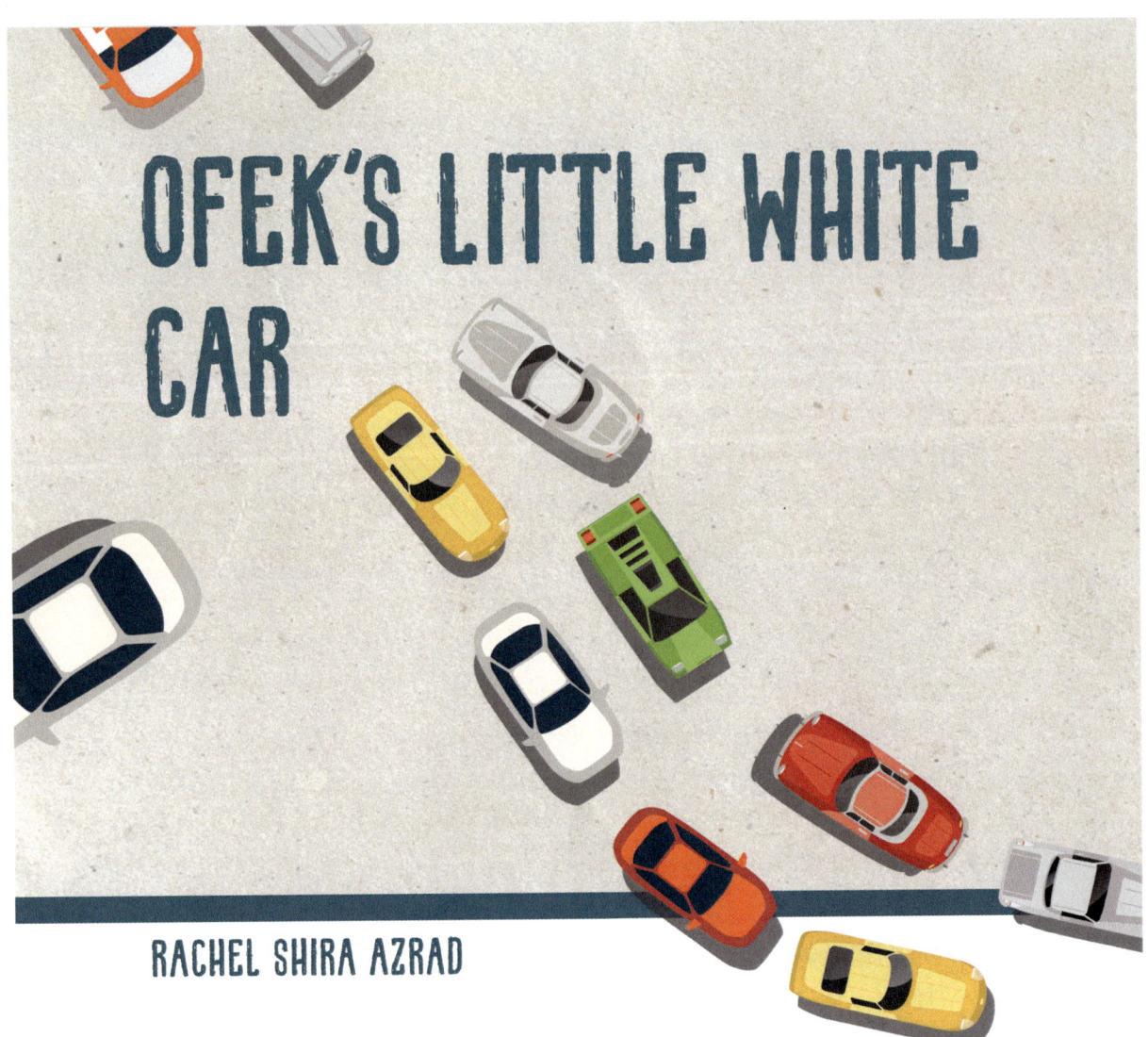

RACHEL SHIRA AZRAD

A long line of cars stretches along the length of the desert road. Inside the cars are people who were dancing all night at a big party, just moments ago. Now there are sirens, and a war has broken out and everyone just wants to get away.

Ofek Livni and his friends are there, in standstill traffic, inside his mother's little white car. They're not getting anywhere.

Police arrive on the scene and urge them to leave: "Get away from here, it's dangerous!" People leave their cars behind and start to run away. But Ofek decides to get back in the car and drive in a different direction. He knows he needs to stay calm now, that's what will help him escape.

On the way he meets Gilad and Neta. He calls out to them: "Hurry up and get in the car!" He calls his dad, Raz, from the road: "They're shooting at us, Abba!" he says. His father listens and says firmly: "First of all, stay calm. And now, listen to me and my voice, and drive exactly where I tell you to go". Ofek listens and Raz expertly guides him through the fields. Raz knows the desert roads very, very well and knows where to go.

Meanwhile, Ofek's small car begins to fill up with people. Even though it can only hold five passengers, Ofek wants to save as many people as possible. There are already six people in the car but when they see two more girls fleeing the scene, Ofek shouts at them: "Come here, get in! We'll make room for you!"

They continue driving through the fields with Ofek's dad, Raz, on the phone. Raz keeps his cool. He's a farmer and he's very familiar with all the ins and outs of the fields. He gives Ofek instructions that only he knows: "Drive along paths where they grow potatoes. Make sure that the fields haven't been watered, so that the car won't get stuck in the mud. Drive in the direction of the sun." Ofek continues on and spies two more people on the road. The car was already stuffed with eight people, but there was still some room in the trunk. Ofek tosses all his stuff out of the trunk of the car and onto the road, and helps the people climb in.

Now they are a group of ten people, in his mom's little white car driving hurriedly to safety. Thankfully, all ten of the passengers made it home, safe and sound – all thanks to Ofek and his dad and their little white car.

EITAN'S DRAWING

HAIM ECKSTEIN

Since the festival of Simchat Torah, Eitan Fish's drawings are no longer strewn all over the house. He was a talented artist; coloring miniature superheroes, sketching highly detailed pictures, and once, he drew on the walls of the entire 'safe room' (*mamad*) at home with illustrated images taken from Winnie the Pooh.

Where did he find the time? Eitan loved developing his talent. Even while learning at the hesder yeshiva in Yerucham and as a combat soldier and commander in the Tank Brigade he continued to draw, and in his vacation time at home he would improve and polish his work. The moment the war broke out though, everything changed. Eitan and his soldiers got organized at lightning speed and headed from their base to the area around the Gaza Strip. Eitan defended the kibbutzim,

helped to fight off the enemy and then prepared to enter into combat in the Gaza Strip itself.

When the forces entered Gaza, the decision was made to leave him in a position outside. Eitan waited for a miracle, hoping that he too would be sent in. When he received permission, he was delighted that he would be given the privilege of participating in the battle.

One day, David, Eitan's father, was organizing the 'messy corner' in the house, which, like most messy corners, was full of loose pages (do you have a corner like this in your house too?). Among the papers he found a new drawing; a soldier with a sword in his hand, holding a child with his other hand, both striding towards a tank. There was no doubt what this drawing portrayed; a soldier who had found a kidnapped child and was returning him home.

The drawing as a whole wasn't complete, but a lot of care and detail had gone into the tank. Only a soldier who served in the Tank Brigade would be able to draw a tank like this one. Later, his army friends would recount that every spare moment during the fighting, Eitan would look around, as though searching, in the hopes he might find one of the kidnapped. The mission to return them was always uppermost in his mind.

Eitan wasn't able to finish what he began. He fought in the north end of the Gaza Strip and saved the lives of dozens of soldiers. An anti-tank missile, which is especially powerful, hit his tank and he was killed. If you look at Eitan's drawing, you'll notice that the sword is taken from the company badge. Eitan dreamed of fulfilling his vision, as well of that of all Am Yisrael – bringing all our kidnapped citizens back home.

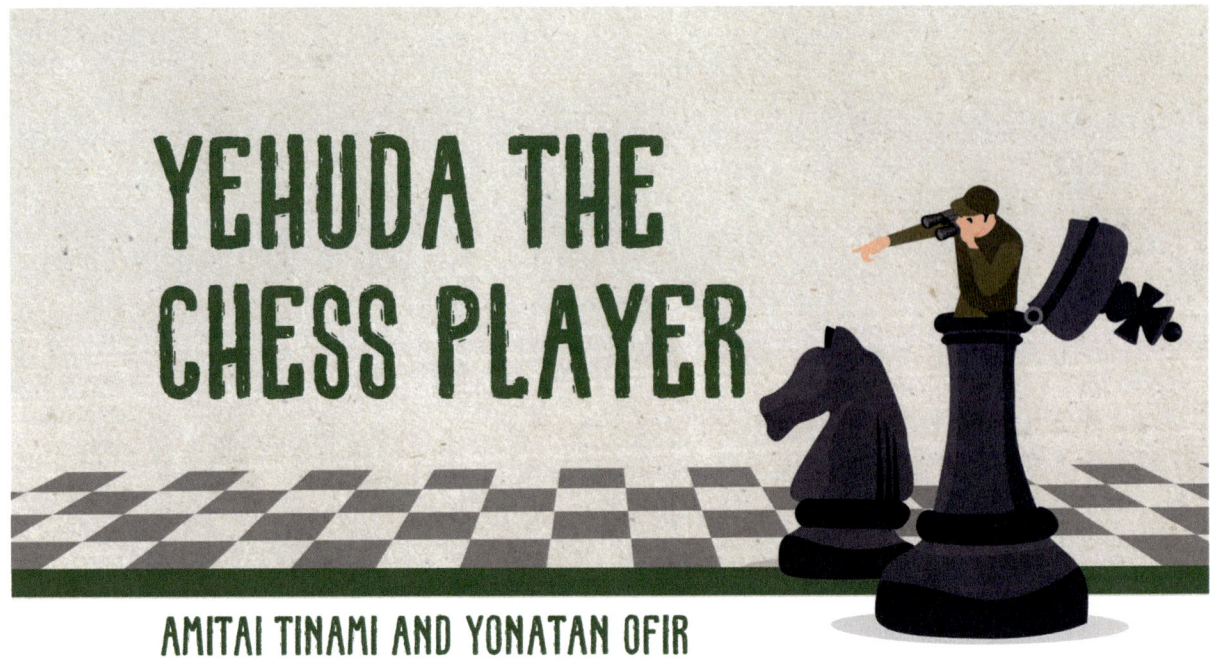

YEHUDA THE CHESS PLAYER

AMITAI TINAMI AND YONATAN OFIR

"Yehuda! Come to dinner!"

"Wait, I just have to beat his queen!"

Yehuda loved to play chess. He was a champion player and competed in Olympic tournaments against famous chess players. He bought his nephews a chess board for Rosh Hashanah, and made sure to teach them how to play correctly: "Always protect the king, and think about what your opponent will do next if you move your piece."

On the morning of October 7th, Yehuda Natan Cohen, a Givati commando company commander, was at home in Shadmot Mehola. When he heard about what was happening in the south, he immediately felt the spirit of the mission filling him. He quickly took off his white shirt, put on his uniform, and left, without even saying goodbye to his nephews.

On the way he picked up all the soldiers in his company and began giving out orders where to go. Yehuda, the chess player, was used to anticipating and thinking several moves ahead; where his soldiers would come from, who would take the lead position and who would cover them from behind.

YEHUDA THE CHESS PLAYER

The Givati commando company under Yehuda's command entered Kibbutz Nahal Oz where there were dozens of terrorists rampaging. They successfully eliminated the terrorists and then proceeded door to door, calling out:

"Open up, it's the IDF. We've come to save you!"

From one of the houses a person called out: "How do we know you are not Hamas?"

Yehuda answered: "I'm Yehuda Cohen, a company commander in the Givati commandos. I've come to help you!"

"If you are a commander, tell me in what year the state was established?"

"1948."

"And who was the first prime minister?"

"David Ben Gurion."

"And who defeated Goliath?"

"David, King of Israel, from the tribe of Judah."

The door opened.

Later, when he spoke to his family, he spoke humbly. He told them that he and his soldiers were guarding the kibbutz and did not mention his many acts of heroism. It was the same with the way he carried his rifle over his shoulder – Yehuda used to place the strap on his other shoulder in order to hide his military rank.

Later in the war Yehuda led his company into Gaza, winning many battles. One day, when the unit was positioned inside a house, Yehuda entered the house opposite them to make sure there was no danger. Upon entering, he found terrorists planning destruction. Before he fell to the enemy, Yehuda managed to warn his soldiers, who eliminated the terrorists. Through his bravery, Commander Yehuda Cohen saved an entire company of soldiers.

CAPTAIN A. DEFENDS OUR SKIES

YONATAN OFIR

"As we ran through the orchards, I felt like one of the Jewish partisans in 1941, who fled from the Nazis to the forests for safety during the Holocaust."

This is how Captain A., from Nes Ziona, describes the moments of escape from the Nova party on October 7th, 2023, when he led around two hundred young people to safety towards Moshav Patish.

A. is a reserve officer in the Israeli Force, who serves in the 'Protective Sword' unit that operates a powerful device, intercepting missiles fired at Israel.

"People were fleeing in droves. We got into the car and started to escape, but the terrorists began to come after us. The situation was quite dangerous and some of the young people

122

who were passing in another car shouted to us to go in the opposite direction."

At the same time, terrorists were roaming the area and there was danger to be found in every direction. There was no chance of escaping, there were long lines of traffic due to the large number of cars trying to flee all at the same time.

"I made a quick decision to leave my car, which had become a trap, and run towards the nearby orchard," A. recounted. "A group of about two hundred completely terrified partygoers followed me and I decided to lead them. I heard continuous gunshots while running but I knew I had to continue. I wasn't even able to stop to take care of any wounded people, I just had to keep going."

A. used Google maps and his experience as an officer to try and lead the group to the city of Ofakim. On the way, he saw an update that the terrorists were already there so he quickly changed direction towards Moshav Patish.

They crossed streams and hid in the bushes. After a long while passed, and the army still had not yet arrived, people began to grow tired. In order to gain their strength back, they began to eat the fruit that they found on the ground of the orchard and drink murky water from the puddles under the trees left from the irrigation system.

About seven hundred meters before reaching the moshav, the residents of Moshav Patish noticed the group and came to rescue them in their vehicles.

After a few days of rest at home, A. joined his reserve unit in the army, protecting the country's skies. With his resourcefulness that day, Captain A. saved around two hundred lives – while in his role in the Air Force, he continues to save countless lives on a daily basis.

HANNAH GIVES US WINGS

YONATAN OFIR

The group of children from Kibbutz Mefalsim sat on a blue carpet in the hotel lobby in Herzliya. Opposite them, on a gray couch, sat Hannah Gofrit – 88 years old, smiling at them.

When Hannah heard that so many children on kibbutzim had been forced to hide from terrorists on October 7th, she decided that her own personal way to help would be to meet with them and share her own experiences. By doing so, maybe she could give them some hope that the future is still bright.

"One day, I had everything and suddenly it disappeared," she told the children. "The house I grew up in, the games, the books and the members of my extended family – all disappeared. Suddenly, there was no home."

"That's what happened to us," the children answered her, and Hannah replied: "That's why I came to talk to you."

About seventy five years ago, the Nazis came to the small

town in Poland where four year-old Hannah lived. Hannah and her mother managed to escape to safety and hide with a Polish family, good people who today we call 'righteous among the nations'. For around two years they lived in the Polish family's house and helped with the household chores, and every time guests came over, Hannah and her mother stepped inside a closet and hid there until any danger had passed.

Six year-old Hannah was afraid of the pitch black darkness inside the closet and the fear that they would be discovered – and it was then she really began to use her imagination.

"I imagined that I was a butterfly with wings, flying back over the town of my childhood. Inside the closet I was not little Hanuchka, hiding and worried, but a free and happy butterfly! Thanks to that vision, I regained the hope that one day life would be good again."

The children of Kibbutz Mefalsim looked at her with eyes full of hope, and they shared their stories with her. Their parents joined them and thanked Hannah, who had also managed to give them, the adults, strength, with her words.

"When I look into the eyes of Holocaust survivors, I feel like I'm looking into the eyes of superheroes – and when I look into your eyes, I feel the same," she told the families of Kibbutz Mefalsim.

Hannah did have a good future waiting for her, she was right. She was blessed with four grandchildren and two great-grandchildren. Her story of survival was published in a children's book called "I wanted to fly like a butterfly", which was translated into seventeen different languages! Hannah and the singer Eliana Tidhar met through the 'Zikaron BaSalon' project, and as a result, the story of Hannah's life transformed into song and performed by Eliana. Hannah, a timeless heroine, who gives us all wings.

GIL'S SMILE OF JOY

EINAT BARZILAI

Genady was only 17 years old when he decided to immigrate to Israel from far-off Russia. It is not at all easy to immigrate alone to another country at such a young age, but Genady was determined. He joined the 'Naaleh' project and enlisted in the army. Eight years later, his brother Yotam joined him and their parents followed later.

During his military service Genady completed his conversion to Judaism, and was in search of a new name; an Israeli name. "What do you say;" Genady asked his friends, "which Hebrew name would suit me?"

Taking into account his lively, happy personality, his friends unanimously agreed; Genady should be called "Gil", the Hebrew word for joy.

Based on his medical tests, Gil was not required to serve in a combat unit. But he didn't let that stop him. He enlisted in the armoured corps and was an excellent soldier; a warrior at heart and a man who above all took care of his friends.

Fifteen years ago, Gil had a serious medical issue, and the army informed him that he would no longer be required to report for reserve duty. They told him to rest and take care of his health. But Gil did not give up.

He remained in the brigade and fought in the Second Lebanon War, in 'Tzuk Eitan' and other military operations, both in Israel's northern region, and in Gaza.

Even when he got sick, Gil wanted to continue contributing to Israel with the same endless commitment and devotion. His friends from the unit say that he always took care of everyone, protected and guarded them before worrying about himself.

Any time there was a need to step out of the tank to get tools or fix something, he immediately jumped in and volunteered.

In the last battle of his life, Gil was part of a long column of armoured vehicles in the dangerous neighbourhoods of northern Gaza. Together with the Givati Brigade, they waged a fierce battle over the Hamas headquarters in the neighbourhood.

The fighting around the headquarters was difficult. Heavy rounds of fire were directed at the vehicles every few minutes. They had to leave the protection of the tank to get a certain tool. The commander explained the situation and Gil immediately shouted and volunteered. "I'm going! You have wives and children!" he said to his friends.

Gil's selfless decision to volunteer to leave the protection of the tank cost him his life.

The friends who were with him said that even when he died, he had a smile on his face. A smile of joy.

ZOHAR SAVES HIS FATHER

HADASSA BEN ARI

The skies are vast and open, the empty road spreads out ahead of a group of friends with their feet on the pedals. Zohar Shachar, fifteen years old, loves his Saturday mornings spent off-road biking. It's the safest time to ride, when the roads are nearly always empty of vehicles. Zohar has been training with a triathlon challenge group in the Gaza Envelope area for the last five years, and this past year his dad, Avi, had joined as well.

The sky was still dark when they left their home on Kibbutz Or HaNer to meet up with friends. They climbed onto their bikes but had barely ridden half a kilometer when the rocket barrage began. They shakily made it to the nearby concrete bomb shelters at the side of the road, but they soon realized that they all needed to get home. Zohar and his dad Avi got into the car with Itai, Zohar's friend. Avi put the pedal to the metal, racing home.

At the entrance to the Chetz Shachor memorial they saw a white pickup truck blocking the road, IDF soldiers standing next to it. Avi headed towards them, shouting: "We're Jews, call an ambulance! We have wounded people here!" The "soldiers" opened fire, revealing themselves as terrorists. Avi, Zohar and Itai were wounded. What could they do? Zohar was the first to realize what was happening and said: "Abba, they're terrorists!" The boy thrust the car into drive, released the handbrake and shouted: "Abba, floor it!" They turned towards the gas station. "Make me a tourniquet", Avi got out of the car on his own, asked the staff at the station for help and they helped bandage him according to his instructions. A while passed but no ambulance arrived. Anna, a friend from the group, offered to take them in her car to go find medical treatment, and they eventually made it to the hospital where they were well cared for.

"I was born on Kibbutz Kfar Etzion", Avi says. "One day before David Ben Gurion declared the establishment of the State, the Arabs in the area set fire to the kibbutz and to all the soldiers who were defending it and protecting the road to Jerusalem. Nineteen years later, when the land was returned to us in the Six Day War, the children of Kfar Etzion returned with Jews from Israel and from abroad, including my parents who made aliyah from America, in order to make this wasteland bloom", Avi connects the past to the present, "today Gush Etzion and Kfar Etzion are flourishing areas. We know that our neighbors don't always love us, but it's our home. We will return to the Gaza Envelope and rebuild. This is our country."

GALI, THE WARRIOR TEEN

REUT GOLDOVSKY

"Turn the sofa over!" The two soldiers from the Duvdevan unit, S. and Y., were in the middle of fighting inside Kibbutz Kfar Aza when a barrage of fire hit them and their comrades. They rushed to take shelter in the nearest house and used furniture to protect themselves and their wounded friends. Chaos reigned over the communications network, with everyone reporting simultaneously about what was happening outside. "Well, this isn't going to work." S. turned off off the noisy communications radio. "You can't understand anything that way. We need to find a way of receiving more organized information."

"I can help," said a voice from behind them. It was 15-year-old Gali Ayalon. The night before, she had come to sleep at her

grandmother's, and when the sirens started, she had locked herself and her family in the safe room. Grandma Liora would not be happy with the mess that the soldiers made in the living room, but at least they were there and could help.

"Here," Gali showed them her cell phone. "All the kibbutz members are posting about their situation on WhatsApp and sending locations. I can put it all together for you so you know what's going on."

The soldiers looked at each other in astonishment. Were they actually going to take orders from a fifteen-and-a-half-year-old girl?

It turns out that the answer was yes.

Gali quickly sent them maps of the kibbutz and began scanning the messages, "Here." She pointed at her screen, "Forces need to get to this neighborhood over here – there are terrorists there." S. ordered some of the soldiers to leave immediately.

Gali worked quietly and calmly. From the thousands of messages coming in, she managed to glean where the terrorists were, where there were wounded people who needed to be rescued, and where there were people who were trapped in their safe rooms. She marked everything on the maps and directed the Duvdevan soldiers to the danger zones while simultaneously reassuring residents and telling them that help was coming. The soldiers and Gali worked together for many long hours, and, with Gali's help, they rescued many families and deterred dozens of terrorists until, finally, Gali and her family were also rescued.

"Gali was literally our operations officer, a warrior in every sense," said S. to her mother when they eventually met. "We're saving a place for her in our unit!"

SALMAN SETS OUT TO WIN

HAIM SCHREIBER

"Load the tanks onto the trucks, now!" Salman Habka, commander of the 53rd Armoured Division barrelled south in his car. The sudden attack in the south of the country was at its peak and Salman lived far away, in the Druze village of Yanukh Jat in the Galilee. "Don't wait for me, just get going. The residents of the Gaza Envelope need immediate help."

During the drive, he planned the battle in his mind and decided to split the forces into teams of two tanks per settlement, to allow them to reach and assist the maximum number of centers.

"53 station commander speaking", Salman addressed his entire battalion on the radio. "When the soldiers fighting hear the noise of the tank treads, it gives them strength. They

know there's strong backup from us. For the residents trapped in their homes, waiting to be rescued, the sound of the tanks tells them we're on the way to save them".

Salman finally hooked up with his tank squad and went into battle, on the way to Be'eri. He had never imagined that he would need to drive a tank along the paths of a kibbutz – and fire on homes! – but the terrorists were hiding inside and there was no choice. Salman was in command and his tank squad began firing. Together, they managed to decimate the enemy, gain back control of the kibbutz and save many, many residents.

The battle ended, but the war had just begun. 53rd Division entered Gaza and their commander Salman was in confident command, leading them. "Now, we're preparing ourselves to smash the enemy", he told his soldiers. "I expect you, and all of Am Yisrael, to continue to be united and resilient, because only together can we win".

One night, Salman heard on the army radio that Golani troops were caught in a hard firefight with numerous terrorists and that some of their vehicles had been hit. "Golani forces need evacuation! Who's coming with me?" he asked, and immediately headed towards them. "There's a big mess there, make sure we aren't firing on IDF troops!" The evacuation was completed successfully, but just then a rocket was fired on the tank and Salman was killed. The brave commander of 53rd Division did exactly what he had always taught his soldiers, and sacrificed his own life for soldiers he didn't even know, out of a total conviction that only by working together would we be able to achieve victory.

NARO, FIGHTER ON ALL FOURS

SHIRA SEGAL

"Naro! Let's sleep!" His handler stifled a smile and turned onto his back. They only had a short time to rest, but Naro the dog didn't care. He wasn't tired, he continued jumping cheerfully and demanding strokes and attention. Why sleep? It's an opportunity to play! This is Naro. Bursting with energy. But make no mistake, Naro is not just any old cute, friendly dog. He's the most agile attack dog in the Oketz ('Sting') Unit, the canine unit of the IDF.

Naro's job is to lead soldiers inside enemy territory and secure them – make sure they're safe. Thanks to his excellent sense of smell, night vision and special combat training, Naro knows how to locate an enemy's hiding place, is super alert when he detects danger and can even surprise and attack terrorists.

Naro and his partner's role is so secret that his handler's name cannot be revealed here, but they are the very best of friends. They enlisted in the IDF at the same time and went

134

through all of their military service together, caring for each other and sometimes it seemed that they could truly read each other's thoughts.

On the morning of October 7th, Naro and his soldier were taken to Kibbutz Kfar Aza, which was under attack. Many terrorists were hiding in houses and ambushing the IDF forces. The soldiers wanted to rush in and save the kibbutz residents, but they didn't know how to distinguish between them and the terrorists.

"We can help!" cried out Naro's handler and knelt beside him. "Naro, I need you to lead us."

The dog straightened up in agreement. They entered the kibbutz with Shayetet soldiers. Naro took the lead and led them along the paths of the kibbutz and inside the houses, always first to warn of danger. Suddenly he started barking and charged forward. A round of shots fired were heard. Terrorists inside the house! Thanks to Naro's warning, nobody was hurt. The soldiers joined the brave dog and fought and fought until they had successfully pushed them back.

Sadly, Naro the warrior dog was killed during the difficult battle. In Naro the warrior dog's merit, so many soldiers received the gift of life. His soldier lost a close and loyal friend and companion, who he misses so much – but one who he's also so, so proud of.

AMICHAI SAVES KIBBUTZ ALUMIM

HAIM SCHREIBER

"It was a holiday, but it was still my job to do shifts in the barn," says Amichai Shacham from Kibbutz Alumim. The night before, the kibbutz had celebrated Simchat Torah in the synagogue, dancing with the books of the Torah as their joy reached all the way up to the sky. The next day, before even the very first rays of sun appeared in the east, Amichai was up and ready to leave the house. "I drank coffee and ate a piece of chocolate cake and on my way to the front door I heard a siren. 'Hurry, everyone into the safe room!' I rushed my children. But suddenly I heard another noise, which is not typical in our area. Gunshots."

Amichai is in a hurry to get to the dairy barn, where the kibbutz workers from Nepal and Thailand were waiting for him. First he grabs bandages when he hears that there are wounded people there. In the meantime, he messages the emergency civilian squad, who are responsible for the safety of all the members of the kibbutz: "Friends, get to the armory quickly and equip yourself."

A friend joins Amichai in treating the wounded when suddenly a loud explosion is heard. "A missile fell on the kibbutz," he messages, but in his gut he also knows: that's not what a missile sounds like. Before a missile explodes, you hear its whistle in the air – and there was no whistle. Amichai raises his eyes towards the west and sees terrorists breaking through Kibbutz Alumim's fence. That's where the loud noise came from. He follows them with his eyes as they approach the first house by the fence. Amichai's house.

Amichai knows his wife and children have locked themselves in the safe room and he has to protect them. In a spur of the moment decision, Amichai shoots in the direction of the terrorists to divert them and his plan works! The terrorists panic and run towards the barn, and then suddenly Amichai is wounded. He seeks medical treatment at the home of Michaela Koretsky, a midwife on the kibbutz, crawling some of the way there, while the emergency squad battles on.

Thanks to the squad's steadfastness, the terrorists abandon their plan to wreak any further damage on Kibbutz Alumim. Although Amichai was injured early in the battle on October 7th, everyone knows that the wisdom and speed with which he acted is what saved Kibbutz Alumim.

ATTENTION TO DETAIL

RACHEL SHIRA AZRAD

Ron Shaked's job in the army is a highly responsible one. He makes sure our soldiers are supplied with all the equipment they need to keep them safe. Ron belongs to a special unit of young people with special needs, called Gedolim BeMadim (Special in Uniform), who volunteer in 70 army bases across Israel. On October 7th, he proved that when your determination outweighs your abilities, anything is possible!

"I can't get the window to close," Ron thought in frustration. He tugged at it again and again, fighting fruitlessly with the stubborn window. As soon as he heard the siren, he ran to the safe room as he had been taught, but he remained upset. Just looking at the window annoyed him. Ron is on the autism spectrum and he needs everything to be done properly.

Perfectly. Others wouldn't understand, but he's really bothered by the improperly shut window.

Ron's studio apartment is in Nahal Oz. He spends his weekends there. The rest of the week he is a volunteer in the IDF, where he works with the Engineering Corps' Logistics Unit. The job suits his personality and skills; he is responsible for ensuring that each soldier leaves with all the necessary equipment. Ron excels at his job because he pays close attention to details and always remembers exactly what each soldier needs. On Saturday morning, October 7th, he was in his apartment. Early in the morning he began hearing sirens and his safe room window wouldn't shut properly.

Ron refuses to give up. He calls his father. "Dad, can you help me? I'm worried. There are non-stop sirens, and I can't seem to close my safe room window." Ron's father lives nearby. He knows what his son is like; if something is bothering him, it needs to be taken seriously. He drives to Ron's house and picks him up. The terrorists are in Ron's parents' neighbourhood as well, but here too, Ron insisted on making sure the door and window were properly shut. Only many hours later, will Ron and his father discover that Ron's attention to detail and caution saved his life twice, both in his studio apartment and at his parents' house!

THE PHOENIX COMPANY

REUT GOLDOVSKY

"I don't understand what the point is. It's total junk, there's no way you'll be able to move it." The officer looked on in amazement as Dan Levitt climbed inside the old tank. The veteran soldier smiled confidently at the younger one: "Let's try – what do we have to lose?"

The idea might sound crazy, but Dan and his friend Erez Sa'adon had made a simple calculation: the army currently lacks active tanks. If they managed to restore the old tanks that stopped being used years ago – the problem could be solved. Dan went around IDF bases looking for armored vehicles that no one was using anymore and tried to get them moving. They put together a technical team to inspect the tanks in depth, they oiled, cleaned, installed spare parts and to everyone's surprise

announced that they had managed to repair – and bring back from the dead – 24 old tanks.

Now all that remained was to find soldiers to drive them.

"We're looking for veteran tank crews who are interested in fighting in Gaza"

Erez and Dan spread the message and within a few days, volunteers from all over the country, and even other countries, showed up at the base. Erez and Dan stood in front of the old iron monsters, a little embarrassed. "Are you serious?! These are our tanks?" said one of the volunteers. "I haven't been in the army for 15 years, but it seems to me that this thing is older than me!" Erez grinned at him and announced the start of training.

After the rust had been removed – from both the vehicles and the guys – the big day finally came: the company set off and crossed the southern border. "Control to all substations, is everyone in position? Over". Each of the tanks confirmed that they were ready. It didn't take long. "Tank 3 to Control, permission to fire?" As soon as the commander authorized it, the gunner fired: the tanks' first operation was a success.

This is how a completely new company in the IDF was formed; one that is made up entirely of reservists who never thought they would wear uniforms again, and tanks that no one thought would fire again: the Phoenix Company, named after the mythical bird that rises in flames from the ashes, reborn every time.

ELISHA HAS NO TIME

ROTEM RESSLER

It was a regular weekday afternoon. Suddenly, strong, happy, singing voices were heard, coming from one of the houses: "Am Yisrael Chai! The Nation of Israel Lives!"

It was the members of the Loewenstern family who went outside to welcome their father Elisha home, returning for a short rest from the fighting in Gaza. He came into the street, traces of the tank's grease still visible on him; black, oily stains on his face, fingers and nails. But through it all he was beaming, with a big smile, followed by a warm embrace.

When Elisha entered the house, he took a long look at the bookshelves. He so missed being immersed in his holy books. He remembered that his wife Hadas, when she packed his bag for the war, had said to him with a sparkle in her eye: "Elisha, all the rabbis who wrote these holy books in your Jewish bookcase –" as she waved her arm towards them excitedly – "Maimonides, the Ramban, the Ritba, the Sha"ch, they all prayed to be in your position now, a place of honor defending the Jewish people and the Holy Land!"

Her clear voice and sparkling eyes remained with him as he rode in the rumbling tank through the alleys of Gaza.

And now her voice, right here next to him, reminded him: "Elisha, were you able to take off your shoes like your mother asked? Do you remember, from the Second Lebanon War, how your feet hurt from you never having time to care of them, and never having time to take off your shoes."

"The truth is, no." Elisha admitted, "I didn't even have one minute to take care of myself or take off my shoes."

To most people, it might sound like an exaggeration to not have a single minute but that was Elisha; he always made sure that every minute was put to good use and if he had a spare moment he would learn from his holy books.

Hadas knew it. "At least now, while you're home," said Hadas, "you have a minute."

A few days later the family celebrated Hanukkah. Elisha had returned to his tank in Gaza and Hadas and the children lit candles at home. That evening the uncles had come to join in lighting the Hanukkah candles and together everyone sang all the verses of "Maoz Tzur". But outside, in the darkness of the night, devastating news awaited them; Elisha had fallen in battle.

Representatives of the army came to console them and be with the family. They said: "We have a picture of Elisha. Someone took a picture of him about two hours before he fell in combat. The soldiers had a minute to rest."

Hadas and the children huddled together, and there he appeared in front of them in the picture; Elisha sitting with his legs in front of him in the tank, in his minute of quiet, studying a holy text by Maimonides... with his shoes on.

REBORN

NAAMA FRENKEL

"This soldier is seriously injured, drive faster!" Noam David, just eighteen years old, not yet in the army, looks down at the soldier in his arms and realizes that she is very badly injured. They race to Soroka Hospital, leaving her in the hands of the dedicated doctors and nurses, and go back to collect more of the wounded. Just a few days later Noam hears – the soldier was called Noa and she survived, thanks to them.

Rewind to the morning of October 7th, when Noam woke up in his second home, the Ein Prat pre-military college where he studies. Bang! The door of his trailer bursts open and Erez, the director of their school, is standing there. He yells out: "Guys! There's a mess going on in the south. Who's joining me to come help?!"

Noam leapt out of bed, got organized and was in the car within minutes. As they drove, the sky filled with black clouds, and the chirping of birds on a Saturday morning was replaced by the echoes of explosions. War was in the air.

Noam and Erez arrived and entered a combat zone, evacuating dozens of wounded all while the battle continued around them. They drove to the hospital and back again and again. When they re-entered the Zikim army base, they heard the faint voice of Michal, a civilian who had come to help soldiers. She had been injured and was asking for water, her arm was wounded. Noam found her water and with a strength he didn't know he had, lifted her into their van, as Erez also loaded the van with more wounded people and again they raced to Soroka hospital, where Michal was saved.

Evening falls. Darkness, the sound of gunfire is relentless – even as they enter Kibbutz Be'eri. They knock on the doors of people's homes: "It's us, it's the IDF!" they shout in Hebrew. They save a mother and baby; a father and grandmother, families. All of these people finally breathe a sigh of relief. They are in good hands, they are alive.

These daring men from Ein Prat, Noam and Erez, knock on another door and there they meet Neta, who is so advanced in her pregnancy she is literally kneeling down on the floor ready to give birth. They drive fast to the hospital, asking her to breathe deeply, they will arrive in just a moment. Just a short time later, Neta is hugging her baby.

Noam suddenly feels everything coming together for him, out of the destruction he has witnessed – life is emerging. A beautiful Israeli baby girl was born. Noam, just eighteen years old and not yet even in the army, looks down at the mother with a baby in her arms, and sees before his very eyes the secret of this nation, which knows how to be reborn, how to bring life, even out of its deepest pain.

I'VE GOT A LITTLE GIRL AT HOME

ROTEM RESSLER

"I'm tired; so completely drained that I may just fall down. I've been working all night, it's unbelievable!" Carmel Efron thought as she fled through the fields, hair flying and exhausted.

Just a few hours earlier, which now seemed like forever ago to her, she had still been working at the party. She'd welcomed the partygoers, made sure that everything was running smoothly, smiling with satisfaction as she saw everyone glittering and floating along with pleasure to the music.

There was a sudden rising and falling noise, and loud booms began to overpower the music.

She immediately realized the sounds were warning sirens, a frightening sound, but she hurried everyone into the safe areas, reassuring them that everything would be alright.

While she sat in the safe room, looking around at all her

friends, the thought flashed through her mind: "What am I doing here? I have a little girl at home. She needs me; I can't stay here. I have to take care of her!". Carmel decided to escape as quickly as possible and left the safe room. At that moment, she didn't realize how fateful her decision would be.

Starting her car, she began driving quickly north through the fields. So many cars were parked in her way, preventing her from continuing onwards. She left the car running with her bag inside, grabbed her phone and began to run.

"I've got a little girl at home. I need to get home to her". Carmel's body surged with power at the thought of her daughter. She imagined her hug and her legs felt strong again.

At one point, when she felt her strength waning, she stopped near a car. A good Samaritan appeared in a large car and picked her up, as well as other people running to escape. They continued on with him until they were forced to get out and hide in the bushes. Carmel and others covered themselves with leaves, hugging one another, trying to keep their spirits up. "Let's smile and take a picture", Carmel suggested, despite the horrible situation.

After a while, rescue forces appeared. Once she was in the car and finally headed to safety, Carmel again felt her total exhaustion. The only thing she wanted was to be in her living room at home, hugging her little girl as tight as possible.

"IMMA!" Her daughter jumped on her and the two hugged. Carmel took a long look at her, with glittering eyes. "Tonight, we'll sleep in the same bed", she stroked her daughter's hair and smiled at her good fortune.

EVERY.
SINGLE.
WORD.

HADASSA BEN ARI

"Do you remember what we talked about today?" Erez Berkowitz, team commander in the Givati Reconnaissance Company, asked his soldiers in the middle of their beret march – a trek that all IDF combat soldiers undergo, at the end of which they receive a beret with a distinctive color that reflects their corps or brigade, ending an important chapter in their training.

"We said that this is not the time to mourn; this is the time to win," he said at the most challenging stage of the hike, when every commander wants to encourage his soldiers. He could no longer hide the secret that he had been keeping for the past few hours.

"Before we set out on our march, I was informed that my older brother was killed in Gaza. I embarked on this important

'beret hike' with you all because my brother would have wanted us to do it, to do it with a smile, as we choose life and action." Erez chose to lead his soldiers, the new generation of warriors, in the steps of his brother Eyal.

"He would have wanted us to smile because that's what he was like. I remember his jokes and the happy atmosphere at our Shabbat table. It's an important trait for a team of warriors and the entire people of Israel."

Eyal was highly talented. He was a medical student, as well as an illustrator of comics and books. "You had every reason to brag, but you never let it blind you." his parents said of him. Occasionally, he would accompany young people suffering from physical disabilities on weekends full of fun. Once, one of his friends called him up to ask him to cheer him up when he was sick. Eyal took him to the desert and drew him against the background of the mountains. After that, they wrote a song together.

He had another unique talent: silence. He was not much of a talker. Every word of his was golden. Although he was very knowledgeable, he didn't try to impress others. Instead, he tried to make people laugh: "My hobbies: Going to a restaurant, ordering an omelet and chicken, and seeing what comes first: the chicken or the egg?" Another example: "I hate people who deliberate over nonsense. Or maybe I don't hate them? I don't know."

Eyal fell in battle in Gaza while on a mission filled with value, caring for the lives of soldiers and other citizens. His mother, Rikki, finds comfort in his heroism, encouraging us all: "We should merit to be worthy, to continue in their ways and be good people."

Y. AND MULO

ROTEM RESSLER

"You've reached your destination", the Waze app announces. Today, I'll tell you a story of someone who reached his destination even though he only made it to the halfway point. How is that even possible?

Y. heard the first siren at home, just as he was about to go for a run. He was a senior commander on the Gaza border, so he immediately began receiving messages and phone calls. "There is an incident in Gaza," he kissed his wife and children. "I'm heading over there and I'll be back at noon."

Y. quickly drove south. Though his destination was the battlefield, he thought that there was another stop he needed to make on his way to the border. He called the security coordinators from all the settlements near the border fence.

"Y.?" Inbal, the head of the security team in Nir Am, was surprised. "A call from you on Shabbat"?

---

* The full name of soldier Y. can not be written, due to the very confidential nature of his job

"Yes Inbal, it's an emergency situation. Go to the armory and start distributing weapons to all the members of the security team. Actually, not just to them. Distribute weapons to everyone. Be ready."

Inbal felt her jaw hardening and hurried to do as he said. Only later would she realize that this call is what had saved the kibbutz.

Bullets flew around Y. and he suddenly felt a sharp pain. He lost control of his vehicle, which swerved to the side and stopped. Y. leaned, wounded, against the steering wheel, in silence. Later he realized that this is what saved his life.

At exactly the same time, a man named Mulo, who had come to Israel from Eritrea, was fleeing from the south in a taxi that was speeding north on the other side of the road. In front of him he saw Y. and his heart would not let him continue. Drop me off here, he told the shocked driver. Mulo quickly approached Y. as the taxi sped away. He took care of him and promised to remain with him until the rescuers came.

"Here are our soldiers!" he said, giving Y. some hope. The soldiers approached with caution, aiming their rifles at him. They thought he was a terrorist.

"What are you doing?!" cried Y. with his remaining strength. "He's helping me!" The soldiers calmed down and called for the rescue forces, who finally arrived to evacuate Y. the heroic officer, and Mulo his savior, a righteous gentile.

Y. is working hard towards a full recovery in a rehabilitation center. Mulo and his children received permission to become official residents of Israel, in thanks for the help he gave Y.

They are on a journey, but have also reached their destination.

YOSEF AND THE DRONE

ALLISON KUPIETZKY

Yosef Malachi Guedalia loved life and lived it to its fullest. He had interesting hobbies including playing competitive frisbee and photographing the beauty of his birthplace – the Land of Israel – with his flying drone that captured photos from the sky. Yosef was always smiling, and his smile widened even more when he met his beloved Senai at a summer camp in America. They got married and built their home together in Israel.

Yosef was 22 years old and served in the Duvdevan unit in the IDF. His skill of flying drones helped him in his military service during various battles against terrorists. He also trained other soldiers on how to use drones to search for people who needed help and bring them to safety.

On October 7th, the holiday of Simchat Torah, Yosef was at prayer with his family in Jerusalem. When he heard that the lives of residents in the south of Israel were being threatened and they needed help, he immediately set out, taking his drone with him so it could fly and look for people in danger. At great speed Yosef arrived at Kibbutz Kfar Aza and managed to save several people. As a soldier of the IDF whose job was to protect Israel, without hesitation and with great courage he returned several times and saved other people.

In one of Yosef's rescue efforts, he was seriously wounded by terrorists. One of the other soldiers immediately sent a drone to locate him, and indeed Yosef was found, and he was brought back, to be laid to rest in Israel. Yosef used the drone to watch over others, and in turn the drone watched over him.

Yosef used his talent, ability, dedication, and courage to save human lives. He not only believed in helping others all his life, but he lived this way until his last day. His brother Asher said that his picture should be displayed in every classroom, so that we can all remember his bravery and learn how to live life from a true hero.

Made in the USA
Las Vegas, NV
29 December 2024

15597204R00098